EMPOWER YOURSELF AT THE OFFICE WITH THIS ESSENTIAL HANDBOOK FOR MANAGING YOUR WORK LIFE

Working With You Is Killing Me

"Crammed full of actionable tips . . . I give this book five stars for building success and emotional comfort in your job."

—Tribune Media Services

"Provides ways to break out of our comfort zone to expand and thrive at work . . . This guide is . . . long on ideas and examples to help you survive."

—*Booklist*

"Empowering . . . a highly practical and easily implemented guide . . . As valuable to readers on the top rungs of the corporate ladder as it is to those near the bottom. Readers in the throes of a work crisis can find a relevant case study to lead them to relief from any situation."

—*Publishers Weekly*

"One way to make your career soar is to get things done with troublesome coworkers. This book tells you how."

—Jeffrey J. Fox, author of *How to Become a Rainmaker*

"Crowley and Elster provide all the tools needed to avoid being taken emotionally hostage in the workplace."

—Lois P. Frankel, PhD, author of *Nice Girls Don't Get Rich* and *Nice Girls Don't Get the Corner Office*

more . . .

"The authors open our eyes by offering very clear and practical solutions to travails with bosses, subordinates, and colleagues. This is the holy grail for architecting a cnflict-free work life!"

—Michael Feiner, author of
The Feiner Points of Leadership

"Packed with profound insights and practical advice that will immediately transform your quality of work and quality of work life."

—Joseph Crenny, coauthor of *Crucial Confrontations*

"Great book! Lots of terrific tools and insights for . . . enhancing relationships both at work and in any area of your life."

—Robert J. Kriegel, PhD, author of
How to Succeed in Business Without Working So Damn Hard

"A wealth of strategies for dealing with coworkers or a boss who is driving you nuts."
—Pam Heim, coauthor of *Hardball for Women*

"A valuable tool for people in every corner of the working world."
—Norma Hurlburt, executive director,
Chamber Music Society of Lincoln Center

"A must read for anyone who has to deal with difficult people or difficult situations at work."

—Lee E. Miller, coauthor of
A Woman's Guide to Successful Negotiating

Working with You Is Killing Me

Freeing Yourself from Emotional Traps at Work

KATHERINE CROWLEY AND **KATHI ELSTER**

BUSINESS
PLUS

NEW YORK   BOSTON

Business Plus
Hachette Book Group
237 Park Avenue
New York, NY 10017

www.HachetteBookGroup.com

Printed in the United States of America

Originally published in hardcover by Hachette Book Group.

First Trade Edition: March 2007

10 9 8

Business Plus is an imprint of Grand Central Publishing.
The Business Plus name and logo are trademarks of Hachette Book Group Inc.

The publisher is not responsible for websites (or their content) that are not owned by the publisher.

The Library of Congress has cataloged the hardcover edition as follows:
Crowley, Katherine.
    Working with you is killing me : freeing yourself from emotional traps at work / Katherine Crowley and Kathi Elster.
        p. cm.

    ISBN 978-0-446-57674-1

    1. Psychology, Industrial. 2. Interpersonal relations. 3. Interpersonal communication. 4. Problem employees. I. Elster, Kathi. II. Title.
    HF5548.8.C685 2006
    650.1'3—dc22   2005022700

ISBN 978-0-446-69849-8 (pbk.)

Design by Nancy Singer Olaguera/ISPN
Text composition by Peng Olaguera/ISPN

This book is dedicated to John S. Crowley,
a man who embodied honesty, integrity,
compassion, and professionalism
through his words and his conduct.

Acknowledgments

We gratefully acknowledge and thank our clients for allowing us to enter their professional and emotional worlds. It has been a privilege to work so closely with so many of you. It takes courage and a willingness to be open and vulnerable. Thank you for trusting us.

We could not have put the time into writing this book without enormous emotional support from David Winkler, Nicole Winkler, and Clif Eddens. Many thanks go to family and friends for your constant interest and encouragement. Thank you, Denyse Thompson, for keeping us organized and thank you, Brynne Damman, for your help.

We extend special thanks to our agent, Elaine Markson, and to Gary Johnson. Thank you, Mark Chimsky, for your tremendous assistance and guidance. Thank you, Donna Ratajczak, for your ideas and input. We are eternally grateful to John Aherne for taking a risk on us. We want to acknowledge Roland Ottewell for his excellent copyediting. Finally, thank you to our editor, Dan Ambrosio, who kept us on task and on time.

Contents

Introduction   xi

1   Change Your Reaction, Change Your Life   1

2   The Business of Boundaries—Protecting Yourself at Work   23

3   If the Role Fits, You Don't Have to Wear It   47

4   Haven't We Met Before? Fatal Attractions at Work   73

5   Managing Up—Taking Control   103

6   Difficult and Extreme Bosses—How to Keep Your Sanity   127

7   Managing Down—Business Parenting   156

8   Corporate Culture—Is This the Right Place for You?   194

Index   223

About the Authors   233

Introduction

If you're reading this page, there's probably someone at work whose behavior drives you crazy. It may be a chaotic coworker, an obnoxious boss, an unruly employee, an inept department, or an impossible client. Whoever it is, interactions with this person or group of people set you off. Their conduct rattles your nerves and upsets your day.

You've probably imagined how great life would be if you could eliminate this workplace irritant. You dream of the day when everyone simply does his or her job without incident and no one invades your space. Dream on.

The fact is that the workplace is a volatile environment inhabited by emotional creatures who often rub each other the wrong way. This is especially true when people are thrown together for many hours in a small space commonly referred to as "the office." Learning how to identify and handle any relationship that holds you back on the job is the purpose of *Working with You Is Killing Me*.

This book will help you "unhook" from any emotional pitfalls in the office and show you how to manage difficult personalities on the job. Each chapter covers a particular brand of potentially distressing behavior in the workplace. Each chapter delivers a framework for solving an emotionally upsetting situation, beginning with figuring out how you may be exacerbating your condition, and concluding with tangible, field-tested actions you can take to transform your experience.

To get you thinking about your workplace challenges, we invite you to take the following quick quiz:

1. Is someone at work killing you?

Put a check mark next to the statements that pertain to you.

_____ Do you have a colleague or boss whose incompetence drives you crazy?

_____ Does a certain department's sloppy way of operating prevent you from doing your job?

_____ Is there a coworker, boss, or customer who wears on your last nerve?

_____ To cope with the stress of your job, do you consume large amounts of food, alcohol, TV, or other mind-altering substances?

If you checked any of these scenarios, you may need to learn the four essential steps to unhooking. Be sure to read Chapter 1, "Change Your Reaction, Change Your Life."

2. Are you caught in a Boundary Busting situation at work?

Put a check mark next to any statements that describe your experience.

_____ Is there someone who eats up your time by constantly arriving late and always missing deadlines?

_____ Do you have a colleague who invades your space by messing up your work area or using your stuff?

_____ Do you ever feel assaulted by the noise that other people make in your office?

_____ Do you feel battered by someone who talks too much and tells you things you really don't want to know?

_____ Do you work with someone whose emotional outbursts (crying, yelling) drain your energy and rattle your nerves?

For help with these uncomfortable issues, learn the boundary guidelines in Chapter 2, "The Business of Boundaries—Protecting Yourself at Work."

3. Check the statement(s) that best describes the role you play at work.

_____ The Dumping Ground—every project ends up on my desk.

_____ The Local Hero—I'm always having to save the day.

_____ The Invisible Man (or Woman)—no one notices me or my contributions.

_____ The Target—I'm always seen as a troublemaker, even when I'm right.

_____ The Entertainer—everyone relies on me to break tension with my humor.

4. Check the statement that describes your biggest workplace problem.

_____ I can't say no whenever someone asks me to take on another responsibility.

_____ I feel responsible for solving other people's personal problems at work.

_____ I frequently clash with people in positions of authority.

_____ Sometimes I wish people took me more seriously.

_____ I have difficulty advocating my point of view at meetings.

_____ I feel that my accomplishments are often ignored or disregarded.

For information about how to break out of constraining roles at work, go to Chapter 3, "If the Role Fits, You Don't Have to Wear It."

5. Do you have a relationship at work that started out with great promise but turned into your worst nightmare?

If so, read the following statements and check the ones that apply.

_____ You constantly rehearse what you want to say to this person in your mind, in your car, and in your sleep.

_____ You find yourself talking about the relationship with friends, family, anyone who will listen.

_____ When you anticipate any interaction with this person you feel anxious, worried, or uneasy.

_____ Conversations with this individual leave you feeling jittery, wound up, overheated, punched out, deflated, or otherwise unhinged.

_____ You feel trapped in a no-win situation.

For skills to manage these toxic relationships, turn to Chapter 4, "Haven't We Met Before? Fatal Attractions at Work."

6. Is your boss someone who . . .

_____ Never takes the time to meet with you, or schedules meetings only to cancel them?

_____ Doesn't tell you what he or she wants, then gets mad at you for not delivering?

_____ Insists that you make decisions in certain areas, only to override the decisions you make?

_____ Expects you to mind-read his or her changing priorities?

For relief from these kinds of experiences, go to Chapter 5, "Managing Up—Taking Control."

7. If you are a manager . . .

_____ Do you hate having to repeat what you want to your subordinates?

_____ Do you wish your staff would just "grow up" and do their jobs?

_____ Do you feel offended when an employee challenges your authority?

_____ Do you see meetings with your staff as time-wasters?

For a course in Managing Down, check out Chapter 7, "Managing Down—Business Parenting."

Who Are We and Why Did We Write This Book?

We are Harvard-trained psychotherapist Katherine Crowley and nationally recognized small business expert Kathi Elster. Published authors, college educators, public speakers, and veteran consultants, we are seasoned guides in the area of professional fulfillment through self-awareness and self-management.

Since 1989, we've helped to retool hundreds of companies by training thousands of individuals in the art of accomplishing their business objectives while navigating the psychological challenges of working with others. We've developed a method for dealing with difficult people and challenging conditions at work. _Working with You Is Killing Me_ is the result of twenty years' worth of research and the combined expertise of a psychotherapist and business strategist.

We think of ourselves as undercover business therapists. We've learned that solving a business problem is easy. Increasing sales, writing a marketing plan, packaging a new product—these are relatively simple things to attain. The tougher, more demanding, more intricate work involves uncovering the emotional traps that managers and their employees fall into and giving them the tools to get out.

Through our extensive experience advising business owners, managers, and employees of every kind, we understand a basic but rarely explored fact: Work, the actual activity of doing a job, is often fairly uncomplicated. It's the *people* at work—bosses, coworkers, clients, and vendors—that present the real challenges.

"I really like my work but my boss drives me crazy. She's constantly giving me things to do, then pulling the rug out from under me."

"Our office manager gives me the third degree every time I request any kind of supplies. How am I supposed to do my job?"

"My assistant is very capable but she takes any correction I make personally. I'm afraid of giving her feedback because she gets mad and freezes me out."

These are common responses frequently voiced in the workplace. While most business books tell readers how to be more productive by managing their external environment, *Working with You Is Killing Me* focuses on the one factor that has the greatest impact on work satisfaction—mastering one's state of mind.

Chapter 1 reveals the essential techniques of "unhooking." It promises that if you can change your *reaction* to distressing circumstances at work, you can change your life. It then lays out the four steps to unhooking: physically, mentally, verbally, and professionally.

Chapter 2 covers the "Business of Boundaries." Here, we identify the many ways that people at work may be invading your physical or personal space, and we explain concrete steps you can take to protect yourself from their behavior.

Chapter 3 zeroes in on the constraining roles people fall into (and get caught in) at work. Find out if you are unconsciously playing a role that prevents you from achieving your goals.

Chapter 4 presents the concept of "Fatal Attractions"—those relationships that start out with a bang but deteriorate into prisons of exasperating interaction; no matter how hard you try you can't win, and somehow you can't break free. In this chapter, we teach you advanced unhooking techniques to help you manage these very challenging workplace associations.

Chapter 5 shows employees how to take charge of their relationships with supervisors by Managing Up, and Chapter 6 investigates the most challenging types of managers—extreme and difficult bosses.

In Chapter 7 managers learn how to handle even the most difficult employees by applying the proven principles of "business parenting."

Finally, Chapter 8 gives you the opportunity to investigate, through self-assessment exercises, what kind of work environment is best for you. You'll evaluate your ethics, values, work behaviors, and lifestyle preferences and compare those with the culture of the company where you're currently employed.

Our hope is that the material in this book will offer relief to anyone facing emotional distress at work. We know that if you read the case studies and apply the tools, your life on the job will improve. You'll spend less time feeling angry, frustrated, thwarted, or otherwise trapped. Your communication skills will improve, and you'll spend less time recovering from work once you leave the office.

Use *Working with You Is Killing Me* as an ongoing guide and reference. Refer back to it as often as you need—whenever a challenging workplace situation arises. This is not a quick-fix book but a handbook for your work life.

Working with You Is Killing Me

1

Change Your Reaction, Change Your Life

Let's explore the two faces of business—the clear, crisp Kodak image that companies present to the outside world, versus the day-to-day reality of working in any company, which is usually messy, complicated, political, and full of emotional traps.

On the surface, business is about making money, delivering goods and services, and producing results. The focus is usually on crunching numbers, meeting deadlines, and increasing sales. We assess individual companies by their empirical facts—profit and loss, cash flow, stock options, and growth potential.

Scratch the rational surface of any company, however, and you uncover a hotbed of emotions: people feeling anxious about performance, angry with coworkers, and misunderstood by management. You find leaders who are burnt out and assistants who are buried in resentment. For example:

Meet Eric, manager of customer service for a fast-growing software company. He's proud of his company's products, but his head starts throbbing whenever he hears from a certain very large account. They're never satisfied with any of the products they've purchased. They claim that the accounting software is too complicated, the database has too many fields, and the time-tracking program doesn't download fast enough. Eric and his staff spend hours addressing their complaints, troubleshooting problems as they arise. "We bust our humps for these guys. As soon as we solve one problem, they call with something else." In between complaints they threaten to leave Eric's company for a better deal. "It's exhausting," Eric sighs. "I can't win."

Jessica is the administrative assistant to the vice president of a small public relations firm. Early each morning, this VP leaves piles of work on Jessica's desk with a note: "Off to scare up more business. Please take care of these things before I return." Jessica arrives at the office, sees the stack of papers on her desk, and immediately feels anxious and overwhelmed. "My boss always gives me more work than I can possibly complete in one day," she complains. "I can't get her to meet with me and prioritize the workload." If Jessica doesn't finish everything, she's labeled "inefficient" or "lacking initiative."

These individuals feel trapped by their circumstances, stuck in a losing game. They're unable to free themselves from a bad situation. Because business calls for unemotional behavior, their feelings remain largely unexpressed and suppressed. They think their options are just to suck it up or quit.

We call the experience of feeling caught in an emotionally distressing situation at work being **hooked**. If you find yourself consistently having a strong negative internal reaction to someone or something in your work environment, you are probably hooked. Emotional hooks vary widely from person to person and job to job. Something as trivial as the nasal tone of a colleague's voice or as weighty as a manager's personality disorder can hook you. A hook can be as simple as a rude remark or as complex as professional sabotage.

If you are a living, breathing, thinking, feeling, normal human being, there's a good chance that you've encountered people and circumstances at work that hook you. In some cases, the incident may generate only mild irritation. In other cases, you may reach a point where you feel like the person or situation is literally killing you.

We've met hardworking individuals who want to be productive and happy at work, but instead feel emotionally trapped in numerous ways. They feel overwhelmed, overworked, underutilized, undermined, disrespected, discounted, interrupted, interrogated, sidetracked, steamrolled, set up, and fed up. Their job descriptions differ, but their experiences are the same.

For most people, earning a living is not an option; it's a requirement. Work eats up more time than any other activity in their lives. At a time when our culture places such emphasis on feeling good, being happy, and having it all, why is it that so many people are dissatisfied at work? Our experience reveals it's largely because they feel trapped, hooked into positions, relationships, and situations that zap their energy, invade their thoughts, and keep them stuck in no-win positions.

The workplace affords numerous opportunities to get hooked, and almost no guidance about how to deal with it. It's appropriate to go to the boss with questions regarding production, accounts receivable, or sales figures. These are nonemotional, factual issues that can be addressed objectively. But when you feel nauseous after a staff meeting or a certain account gives you a migraine, where do you turn?

Take Susan, a marketing executive for a large financial services company. It's Thursday morning and she's sitting at the weekly staff meeting where the departments are giving their reports. Susan's colleague Tracy unabashedly takes credit for a brilliant promotion idea that Susan had originated.

Susan feels a flash of heat surging through her body. Her face turns red. Her eyelid starts to twitch. Her hearing fades. All she can think about is how she'd like to strangle Tracy. Instead of speaking up or joining the meeting, Susan mentally checks out.

Susan just got hooked. Her reaction to Tracy's behavior was to seethe with anger and stop participating. While Susan's response is understandable, getting caught in her own anger doesn't help her situation. In fact, tuning out makes her appear uninterested in the very idea she created.

Susan's experience at her company's staff meeting is not unique. In fact, it's commonplace. The normal reaction when someone else's behavior upsets you is to blame your internal responses on that individual's conduct. As Tony Soprano would say before shooting his latest betrayer, "Look what you made me do!"

In many cases, your response to the situation may make perfect sense. Vicious office gossip *is* infuriating. An incompetent coworker *can* be maddening. When a diva of a customer won't return calls it *does* feel insulting. But, as with Susan, your righteous indignation doesn't improve anything. It just keeps you hooked.

There is a way out. You don't necessarily have to kill anyone or quit your job. You can stay right where you are and still have a different, more satisfying experience. We've helped thousands of people like Eric, Jessica, and Susan transform their workplace from a den of personal frustration to an arena for professional development.

In our work with executives, managers, and employees from every industry, we've learned that the most effective way to resolve interpersonal problems in the workplace is to approach the situation from the inside out. We teach our clients that the key to dealing effectively with difficult people and situations at work is to manage our *internal responses* first. By internal response we mean the automatic reaction that someone else's behavior triggers inside of you. People lose it in different ways. You may heat up, blow up, shut down, freeze up, or go into a tailspin.

If you can change your reaction, you'll change your life.

We call the activity of changing your reaction to emotionally upsetting circumstances at work **unhooking**. Unhooking is a system that gives you tools for managing yourself and taking charge of your work life. Whether you feel caught in political crossfire, trapped by a difficult coworker, or held hostage by the antics of a certain department, you can unhook and take practical steps to change your behavior and create a different result.

Unhooking provides an alternative to your automatic reactions: You can despise the malicious office gossip or you can unhook by setting clear boundaries and showing a lack of interest. You can judge the incompetent coworker or you can unhook by lowering your expectations and avoiding the negative impact of that person's ineptitude. You can feel insulted by the customer who won't return your calls or you can unhook—take it in stride and accept it as part of doing business.

There are four essential steps to unhooking.

Step 1—Unhook physically

Step 2—Unhook mentally

Step 3—Unhook verbally

Step 4—Unhook with a business tool

The first two steps, unhooking physically and mentally, help you release negative emotions and calm down your system. The second two steps, unhooking verbally and with a business tool, involve taking actions to change your experience. To show you how unhooking works, we return to Susan and offer a revised scenario:

Sitting at the same meeting, Tracy proudly takes credit for Susan's brilliant promotion idea. Susan feels herself reacting—feels the surge of heat through her body, feels her face redden, her brow twitch. She realizes, "I just got hooked." What Susan needs to do now is to unhook; she needs to change her reaction to Tracy's sabotaging behavior.

Unhook physically: Susan breathes deeply to calm herself down, release her anger, and check back into the meeting.

Unhook mentally: Susan tells herself not to be intimidated by Tracy's behavior; she can find a way to be heard.

Unhook verbally: Susan speaks up: "When I first ran this idea by Tracy, we both got excited about it."

Unhook with a business tool: Susan writes and distributes an e-mail summarizing the results of the meeting and clarifying the fact that the promotion idea originated with her: ". . . *I'm glad that my promotion idea received such a positive response from the rest of the team. I look forward to working with everyone to develop it further.*"

Like Susan, once you realize that you're hooked, you can begin taking responsibility for your own reactions. You can use our four-pronged approach to free yourself from any person or situation that causes you emotional turmoil. Unhooking takes practice, but it works.

Here is a more detailed description of how to employ each step in the unhooking process:

Unhook physically: Calm the body and release unwanted negative energy so that you can see your situation more clearly. Physical unhooking begins with focusing on your breath, because emotional discomfort normally produces shallow breathing, which inhibits your ability to think clearly. As you consciously breathe in deeply and gently, you can also scan your body to determine how and where you may be holding tension.

In some cases, unhooking physically requires releasing energy through physical activity—you may need to walk around the block, punch pillows, engage in rigorous exercise, take a boxing class, or get a massage. The more extreme your emotional response is to your external circumstances, the more vigorous your physical unhooking activities need to be. The goal is to release pent-up energy and quiet your nervous system so you can approach the problem with a sense of control.

For example, you come out of a business meeting feeling upset because your boss unfairly bashed you in front of your peers. You know you need to cool down. You look at your options. If you can grab a brisk five-minute walk outside, you go for it. If you can't go outside, you go to the bathroom, splash your face with cold water, and BREATHE.

We know that when you're in a distressed physical state, the last thing you want to do is calm down. You'd probably prefer to punch someone's lights out or tender your resignation. The last thing you want to hear is, "Take a breath, relax, go for a walk." But the fact is that if you want to change your life at work, you have to focus on relaxing physically first.

Many places of employment understand the importance of exercise. They may offer in-house yoga, stretching, aerobics, or running. Your company may offer discounted memberships to health clubs or exercise programs nearby. Check out what is available to you, and find the form of physical unhooking that works best for you.

We will use the term **unhook physically** repeatedly in this book. It refers to healthy ways of physically releasing negative energy, and covers a wide range of activities, from exercise to deep breathing to splashing water on your face. It's important to distinguish between healthy and unhealthy forms of releasing negative energy. For many of us, our natural instinct when feeling distraught is to overindulge in one of the following: food, sleep, cigarettes, alcohol, drugs, or television. These activities only eliminate stress for a short period. They do not solve or resolve the problem. In fact, they can cause other problems such as depression, anxiety, alcoholism, obesity, or ulcers. What we are suggesting here is the healthy alternative to alleviating emotional discomfort in the workplace. We can't overemphasize the importance of finding healthy ways to unhook physically.

COUNT TO SIX

Here's an easy method for calming your body through breathing. Breathe in for three counts, hold it for three counts, and breathe out for six counts. Repeat this exercise until you feel your system cooling down.

Unhook mentally: Unhooking mentally is the internal version of talking yourself down off the ledge. It involves looking at your difficult situation from a fresh perspective. The goal is to view your circumstances objectively and see what practical options are available. The rational part of your brain must help the emotional part of your brain cool off, calm down, and strategize. Mental unhooking begins with a quick inventory of the situation:

- What's happening here?
- What are the facts of the situation?
- What's their part?
- What's my part?
- What are my options?

As you can imagine, that fourth question, "What's my part?" is usually the toughest to answer. When a situation causes emotional distress, your natural reaction is to blame the primary offenders, not yourself. Still, if you can uncover your part in the difficult situation, you can also find your point of leverage.

Let's illustrate what we mean: If you're a very nice person, you may not set firm boundaries with people at work. You may find that coworkers, bosses, and customers take advantage of you. Your part in these scenarios would be your inability to draw the line and establish clear limits within these relationships. You have a hard time saying no and sticking to it. Once you discover your role—trouble setting boundaries—you can commit to learning boundary-setting skills.

Once your mind can see the situation from a clearer point of view, you can prepare to take action. For example, say you go to the department file room to ask the clerk for a particular report. She snaps at you: "I have more important people than you waiting for files. I'll get your document when it suits me." You feel your chest tighten. This isn't the first time this person has chewed you out. You don't like her attitude. Instead of striking back, you begin to unhook mentally. You ask yourself:

- What's happening? *The file clerk just snapped at me (again).*

- What are the facts? *I need that report and she doesn't want to get it for me.*
- What's her part? *She's moody and not very happy at her job. Everyone is afraid of her.*
- What's my part? *I take her anger personally. It stops me from completing my own responsibilities.*
- What are my options? *I can stop personalizing her bad behavior. This person isn't angry with me, she's just angry. I can acknowledge her feelings of being overworked and still find ways to get the chart.*

Unhook verbally: Find the words (or sometimes the silence) to protect yourself and get out of a workplace trap. Verbal unhooking may involve finding ways to say no without jeopardizing your job, speaking up when you feel overlooked, or tolerating your boss's temporary silence immediately after you ask for a raise.

To unhook verbally, you must be willing to focus on your overall goal in any situation rather than staying stuck in the petty details. It's a high-road approach to communicating. The goal is to express your ideas and convey information in a manner that resolves problems rather than perpetuating them.

High-road communication contains no judgment, no anger, and no accusations. It includes taking responsibility for your side of the situation.

- Low road—"You messed up again."
- High road—"How are we going to solve this problem?"
- Low road—"Can't you do anything right?"
- High road—"We need to create a system for quality control."

Taking the high road isn't about smoothing things over or being too nice. It's about communicating effectively, in a way that enables the listener to hear you and consider your ideas. It creates a bridge (not a wedge) between you and the person whose behavior is driving you crazy.

For example, say you work for a company where the design

department is continually late delivering samples to your production department. You sit for hours waiting for their prototypes. By the time you receive them, you have to work overtime fabricating enough product for shipping. Instead of fueling your own frustration regarding the design department's poor planning, you unhook verbally. You approach the senior designer and say, "How can I help you get your samples out on time? I have workers that can assist you or we can requisition the help you need."

Unhook with a business tool: A business tool is any standard procedure or written document used in a business setting. It includes contracts, timesheets, job descriptions, memos, performance reviews, company policies and procedures, and other forms of documentation. Business tools help depersonalize challenging situations by providing objective ways to track events and measure performance. To unhook, survey the business tools available to you and identify which ones can help improve your situation.

For example, suppose you're a manager who is constantly irritated by your employee's sloppy work habits. He arrives late, hands you half-baked reports, and spends hours playing computer games at his desk. Instead of letting his poor work ethic drive you crazy, you can unhook using business tools. First, you can refer to his **job description**. Is this person fulfilling the responsibilities of the job? If not, you can devise **performance standards** that spell out the quantity and quality of the work you expect from this subordinate. You can **document** any incident wherein he produces substandard work. Finally, you can give regular **performance reviews** where you evaluate every aspect of his behavior on the job.

Your Business Toolbox

There are a number of professional tools available to you that can move any situation out of the emotional realm and put it back into a business context. Even the most complex interpersonal traps can be improved if you employ the right business instrument.

An unruly client can be put in his place if you refer to and implement your company's customer policies. Careful documentation and cc'd e-mails can expose the covert actions of a cutthroat coworker.

Selecting and utilizing the right business tool for your condition requires strategic thinking. You have to consider the players involved and determine which tactic will produce the best results. You don't want to overwhelm anyone with too much documentation or lengthy, rambling reports.

The following is a list of business tools available to you for unhooking. If your circumstances seem too complicated for these techniques, never fear. In later chapters we'll reveal advanced unhooking techniques for the really tough scenarios.

If you work for a small company, standard workplace documents such as job descriptions, performance reviews, and company policies and procedures may not exist. You may want to help develop these systems for your employer. If you're working for a large, established corporation, all of the following business tools should be readily available.

1. Job descriptions—detailed explanations of the responsibilities that any job entails

   • Managers can refer to these to hold an individual accountable for performing the duties of a job.
   • Employees can refer to these when they need to define the limits of what should be expected of them.

2. Employee expectations/goals—concrete, measurable benchmarks for performance
   A salesperson's job description may say, "Sell xyz product." The company's expectations/goals should specify, "Sell $3 million worth of xyz product by April 1."

   • Managers can use these to evaluate performance.
   • Employees can draw on these to monitor their own success, and to know how they're being evaluated.

3. Performance reviews—quarterly, semiannual, or annual appraisals of an employee's overall job performance

    -   Employers and managers can use these to tell employees where they need improvement.
    -   Employees can use these to substantiate promotions and raises.

4. Policies and procedures—also known as an employee handbook, a document that delineates the company's overall code of conduct

    -   Both managers and employees can refer to this as a guideline for defining acceptable and unacceptable behavior.

5. Disciplinary action forms—written reports that document unsatisfactory employee behavior and forewarn the employee of possible termination

    -   Employers and managers can use these to let employees know when their behavior has crossed the line or their job is in jeopardy.

6. Memos, e-mails, letters—any form of written correspondence

    -   Both managers and employees can use these different modes of communication to report a success, follow up a meeting, clarify a misunderstanding, lay out a plan, or convey other kinds of important information.

7. Meeting agendas—formal lists of topics to be discussed at meetings

    -   Managers can refer to their agendas to keep their meetings focused and on track.
    -   Employees can bring their own agendas to meetings with coworkers and supervisors to guide the conversation and cover important points.

8. Documentation—a written record that provides factual information regarding an event, including time, date, and a description of the incident

- Both managers and employees can draw on this tool to gather data regarding any situation that has them hooked.

How to Identify a Hook Before It Reels You In

Most people become hooked before they even know what's happened to them. Identifying potential hooks *before* they grab you takes years of practice. Still, you can realize you're hooked before it wreaks havoc on your professional life. The sooner you recognize that someone else's behavior is hooking you, the sooner you can do something about it.

Are You Hooked?

Individuals respond to emotionally upsetting circumstances differently. Some people react **physically**. Their bodies send them physical signals that indicate the presence of emotional distress. If you are someone who gets hooked physically, you may experience one or more of the following symptoms: clenched teeth, stiff neck, tension headaches, tight chest, overheating, chills, stomach pain or nausea, shortness of breath, tingling arms, backaches, muscle spasms, facial twitches, insomnia, or fatigue.

> *Harvey works for the leasing department of a major car manu- facturer. He hears his phone ring, looks at the caller ID, and experiences a tightening sensation in his upper back. It's Mr. Sullivan (also known as Mr. Talktoomuch), his neediest lease- holder. Harvey checks the time on his desk clock: 2:15 p.m. He's got an important meeting with his supervisor scheduled for 2:30 p.m. The pain in Harvey's back begins to creep up to his neck because he knows that Mr. Sullivan will want more than fifteen minutes of his time. By 2:40 p.m., the pain in Harvey's neck is sharp and persistent. He manages to get Mr. Sullivan off the phone and sprints to his supervisor's office.*

Some people react to hooks by experiencing **emotional** symp- toms. They feel strong negative emotions such as anger, fear, panic, anxiety, embarrassment, confusion, depression, repulsion, helplessness, or despair. If you are an emotional reactor, you may respond to people and circumstances that drive you crazy with emotional outbursts such as uncontrollable rage, sudden tears, or inappropriate laughter. Emotional reactions to hooks are often accompanied by physical reactions.

Cara is the personal assistant to a well-known interior designer, Erica Payne. When Erica saunters into the office, Cara immediately feels a wave of anxiety. She knows that Erica will seek and find something to criticize. Yesterday, Erica singled out Cara in front of the other employees. She reprimanded her for organizing the swatches incorrectly. "Didn't they teach you anything in college?" Erica chided. Cara felt embarrassed and furious at the same time. Ever since Cara started working for Erica, her moods have taken a downward turn. Every time she even thinks about work, she starts to feel depressed.

Another common reaction to hooks in the workplace involves unproductive **mental** activity. A difficult relationship or scenario on the job may generate obsessive thinking, spacing out, constant distraction, paranoia, revenge fantasies, forgetfulness, or an inability to concentrate. When you're mentally hooked, your mind works overtime in an attempt to solve the disturbing situation.

Jose recently got promoted to head of receivables for a bottle manufacturer. Because he's new to this detail-oriented position, he requires long periods of concentration. Jose has two chatty coworkers who sit right behind him. They talk to each other all day long. Sometimes their conversations are work-related, sometimes they aren't. Their incessant chattering feels like a swarm of gnats buzzing around his head. Jose can't concentrate long enough to complete his assignments. Either their noise distracts him, or he obsesses about how to shut them up. Either way, he can't get their voices out of his head.

Whether you are someone who gets hooked physically, emotionally, or mentally, the sooner you can establish that a person or situation at work has you hooked, the sooner you can begin to address it. During the course of your work week, notice which people and circumstances elicit positive internal responses in you and which ones leave you feeling tense, churned up, or defeated. See if you can identify who and what hooks you. From there, you can apply our four-pronged process and begin to unhook.

The following stories illustrate how unhooking works from start to finish. Read about Glenn and Tom. See how they discover that they are hooked, and how they unhook from their challenging situations. Then conduct your own unhooking exercise using the assessment at the end of this chapter.

Glenn's Story

Glenn is a senior software designer for a West Coast software company. His life changed the day his boss, Arthur, left the company for a new position. Arthur's hands-off management style really worked for Glenn. Arthur allowed Glenn to design new software programs with minimal interference. Together they produced a wide range of new products.

Arthur's replacement, Mike, works very differently. Within the first week of his arrival, the new VP of software development meets with Glenn. "I believe in hands-on management," Mike explains. "I don't accept sloppy work and I require detailed daily reports from my employees regarding the status of their projects."

At the end of each business day, Mike insists on meeting with Glenn to go over his report, point by point. He questions Glenn regarding the design decisions he makes. Glenn is appalled to find himself defending his software models.

After just one month under Mike's management style, Glenn feels tired, irritated, undermined, and frustrated. His new boss is driving him crazy. Glenn believes that the reports are a waste of his time, and he resents having to justify his design choices. "I'm so busy substantiating my work, I'm not able to accomplish anything."

For several weeks, Glenn obsesses about his new situation. He can't stop thinking about Mike, talking about Mike, complaining about Mike. In his mind, he plays and replays imagined conversations where he summons the courage to tell Mike off and prove him wrong.

Glenn talks about Mike to his wife for hours. When his wife can't listen anymore he calls his best friend, Hal. Even Glenn's running buddy, Fitz, gets an earful. Finally, Glenn's fifteen-year-old son walks into the living room and casually remarks, "Dad, you're out of control. This guy Mike is running your life. Chill out."

In that moment, Glenn realizes he's hooked. His negative feelings and thoughts about his new manager are making him miserable. Before Mike became his boss, Glenn enjoyed his work and appreciated his employer. Now he constantly feels frustrated and upset. Instead of focusing on Mike's shortcomings, Glenn decides to try changing his own reaction first. He begins the unhooking process.

Unhook physically: Glenn goes for a really long run. This time, he runs by himself. Instead of obsessing about Mike, he focuses on releasing pent-up energy and clearing his mind.

Unhook mentally: After his run, Glenn sits down and takes an inventory of his situation:

- What's happening here? *I have a new boss, and I don't like his management style.*
- What are the facts? *Mike insists on daily meetings and regular reports. I consider these a waste of my time.*
- What's his part? *Mike believes in hands-on management, and he won't let me do things the way I used to.*

- What's my part? *I don't like change and I refuse to see the value in Mike's approach to designing software.*
- What are my options? *I can continue to be unhappy with Mike's style, or I can give it a chance. I can also look for another job.*

After taking the inventory, Mike admits to himself that even though he and Arthur created a lot of imaginative software, each program usually contained numerous bugs. These design glitches took months to solve before the software could be mass-produced.

Glenn decides that he can at least experiment with Mike's more cautious approach to software development. For the next few months, he can adjust his attitude about the daily status meetings. He can adhere to Mike's method and see if it generates positive results. If Glenn is still unhappy after three months, he can circulate his résumé.

Unhook verbally: Glenn finds the words to let Mike know he's ready to really cooperate. "I respect your desire to create a higher-quality product. It's taking me a while to get used to the new routine, but I'm behind you."

Unhook with a business tool: Glenn meets with Mike every day for three months and goes over his reports. As the quality of his work improves and the bugs disappear, he asks Mike if they can meet a little less frequently—weekly rather than daily—so that he has more time to design software.

Tom's Story

For ten years, Tom has worked as a reference librarian for a top university. Recently, he received a promotion to director of the entire reference department. As soon as Tom assumed his new position, Denise, his coworker of many years, began to act strangely toward him. Before the promotion, they enjoyed a warm friendship. But now Denise is cold and icy.

Denise won't talk to Tom or look in his direction. At lunch, she sits with her back to him. At meetings, she glares when he asks her a question. For reasons Tom doesn't understand, his former friend resents him and treats him with contempt.

Afraid of exacerbating the situation, Tom responds to Denise's cold shoulder by avoiding her. He begins to dread going to work. One day, Tom walks by Denise and George, another reference librarian. He overhears Denise putting him down. "Tom is a study in incompetent leadership. I could run the department more efficiently with my eyes closed."

Tom feels his blood boil. He wants to kill Denise. He imagines himself "accidentally" pushing a bookcase on top of her. He realizes that he is totally hooked by her hostile behavior. Instead of acting out his violent fantasy, Tom leaves the building and begins to unhook.

Unhook physically: Tom takes a brisk walk around campus. He starts to have a conversation with himself. He's tired of feeling bullied by Denise. He needs to sort through his options.

Unhook mentally: Tom takes an inventory of his situation:

- What's happening here? *I got promoted and my former coworker is treating me poorly.*
- What are the facts of the situation? *I am her boss. She reports to me. She was my friend. Now she won't talk to me.*
- What is her part? *She's angry and treating me with contempt.*
- What's my part? *I'm afraid to confront her. By remaining silent, I tacitly permit her unprofessional behavior.*
- What are my options? *I can continue to let her terrorize me, or I can start setting boundaries by clarifying the behaviors that are acceptable and unacceptable to me.*

After taking the inventory, Tom establishes that he's been allowing Denise to control their relationship. Technically, he is her boss. He has the power to confront her rude conduct. His silence allows Denise to continue acting out.

Unhook verbally: Tom returns to the library, walks up to Denise, and says, "We need to talk. Meet me in a half hour in my office." If Denise challenges him he can say, "This meeting isn't optional. I'll see you in my office."

Unhook with a business tool: Back in his office, Tom sits down and begins to document specific incidents during the past two weeks where Denise refused to answer him, ridiculed him in front of coworkers, or withheld information. He prints up a copy for both of them. When Denise arrives for their meeting, he hands her the list. He clearly states his position: "This is what I've experienced in the last couple of weeks from you. It's unacceptable behavior. I'm going to put this document in your HR file. It will be part of your permanent record unless you improve within the next week." Tom completes the meeting by saying, "We've gotten along well in the past. I'd like to return to having a positive work environment here."

Putting It All Together—Your Personal Unhooking Assessment

Now it's your turn to practice unhooking. Pick one person or situation in your workplace that has you hooked, and complete the following assessment.

1. **Describe the overall situation. Who is involved and what keeps happening?**

   _____

   _____

   _____

   _____

   _____

2. List the symptoms you're exhibiting that indicate you're hooked:

Physical: How is your body reacting? Where is the discomfort?

_____

_____

Emotional: What uncomfortable feelings are you experiencing?

_____

_____

Mental: What thoughts are invading your day-to-day activities?

_____

_____

3. Unhook:

Physically: List the actions you can take to release energy and calm down your body.

_____

_____

_____

Mentally: Take a mental inventory of your situation:

• What's happening here? _____

_____

- What are the facts of the situation? _____

_____

- What's their part? _____

_____

- What's my part? _____

_____

- What are my options? _____

_____

Verbally: What can you say that will resolve the problem rather than perpetuate it?

_____

_____

_____

Business tool: What business tools can depersonalize this challenging situation and provide ways to track events and measure performance?

_____

_____

_____

Repeat this process with each hook you encounter.

UNHOOKING AT A GLANCE

Warning Signs That You May Be Hooked

Physical—clenched teeth, stiff neck, tension headaches, tight chest, overheating, chills, stomach pain or nausea, shortness of breath, tingling arms, backaches, muscle spasms, facial twitches, insomnia, or fatigue

Emotional—anger, fear, panic, anxiety, embarrassment, confusion, depression, repulsion, helplessness, or despair

Mental—obsessive thinking, spacing out, constant distraction, paranoia, revenge fantasies, forgetfulness, or an inability to concentrate

Four-Pronged Unhooking Technique

Unhook physically: Breathe, exercise, calm and release your physical energy.

Unhook mentally: Ask yourself, "What's happening here?" Stick to the facts.

Unhook verbally: Decide what you will say to resolve the problem.

Unhook with a business tool: Scan your business toolbox and pick the best one.

2

The Business of Boundaries— Protecting Yourself at Work

Now that we've introduced the general principles of unhooking, it's time to apply these principles to specific danger zones. We begin with workplace boundaries—those invisible lines that define our physical and personal territory. In the workplace, interpersonal boundaries are frequently crossed.

BOUNDARY GUIDELINES

If you are continually angry, upset, or complaining about someone or something, you probably need to set a boundary.

When setting a limit with someone, state it clearly, without anger, in as few words as possible.

Don't set a boundary unless you're prepared to maintain it.

Glenda is having a problem with her coworker Sam, a sales rep for financial products. Sam works in the bullpen with other salespeople. "The Pen" consists of a large open workspace where each rep has a desk, a computer, a phone, and virtually no privacy. As the administrative assistant to the VP of sales, Glenda's workspace is more secluded—she's got a cubicle right next to her boss's corner office at the far end of the floor.

Glenda's current situation began innocently enough. Two months ago, Sam approached her and asked if he could use her phone during lunch hour to make a personal phone call. "You know how loud it is in that pen," he confided. "I don't want everyone knowing my business. If I use my cell, I have to go outside." Because Glenda has always felt a little guilty about having a private cubicle and because she likes Sam, she said yes.

Eight weeks later, Glenda can't get Sam out of her space. Every afternoon, as she returns from lunch, she finds evidence of Sam's presence in her cubicle. She discovers crumbs on her desk, soda cans in her wastebasket, doodles on her notepad. As she sponges off her desk and drops Sam's cans in the recycling bin, she imagines confronting him: "How dare you come into my cubicle and use my phone without asking me!" Upon further reflection, however, she stops herself. "Maybe I'm being too possessive of my space," she reasons. "It must be tough for Sam to be surrounded by other people all day."

One afternoon, Glenda returns from her lunch break to find Sam staked out in her cubicle. She stares in disbelief as her coworker leans back in her chair, props his feet up on her desk, and holds court on her phone. As Sam becomes aware of Glenda's presence, he smiles and puts up his index finger to signal "one more minute." Glenda backs away. Twenty minutes later, she finds herself lurking outside her own cubicle. Her blood starts to boil. She feels angry and used.

Glenda is hooked into an interpersonal dilemma at work. What began as a kind gesture toward her coworker has developed into a spatial nightmare. When Glenda said yes to Sam's request to use her phone two months ago, she assumed she was granting a one-time favor. Sam, on the other hand, interpreted Glenda's yes as a green light to inhabit her cubicle whenever she vacated it.

While it may be tempting to judge Sam for taking such liberties, the real issue involves **differing interpersonal boundaries**. Sam's sense of personal space differs greatly from Glenda's. He feels perfectly comfortable using his colleague's property as if it were his own. Glenda feels invaded by Sam's lax attitude toward her personal space. For her to unhook, she must be willing to draw the line. She must clearly communicate her limits when it comes to Sam using her space.

Boundaries are the lines or parameters that define territory and protect its inhabitants. Geographic boundaries are visible and therefore easy to recognize. Signs tell you when you're leaving one state and entering another. Borders clearly define the boundaries between countries. Landowners delineate their property by using gates, fences, and other kinds of physical indicators.

Interpersonal boundaries are the lines or parameters that define and protect the physical, emotional, and psychological territory between individuals. They are far more difficult than geographic boundaries to discern. First, interpersonal boundaries are invisible. That means you only know you've crossed someone's boundary if they inform you. Second, interpersonal boundaries differ from one person to another. Each person has evolved a unique set of boundaries and rules:

- Your boss may think it's fine to hand you a report at 5:30 p.m. expecting you to complete it before you leave at 6 p.m., while you see his last-minute request as an infringement on your time.
- A colleague may see nothing wrong with listening in on your phone conversations, while you view that as an invasion of privacy.
- One employee may freely divulge the intimate details of a new romance, while another may consider the discussion of personal matters off-limits at work.

Because interpersonal boundaries are imperceptible to the human eye, and because they differ from person to person, they have to be communicated. Part of any job involves defining and expressing your own interpersonal boundaries as well as discovering and respecting those of your coworkers.

Consider your boundaries in each of the following areas:

Time

Time is a huge arena for boundary differences. As you've probably noticed, individuals vary widely in how they perceive time and how they relate to it. There are people who think that a 10 a.m. appointment means anywhere between 10 and 10:45. Some people habitually wait until the last minute to complete their work assignments. There are people who show up early for work and arrive early to every appointment. Some people never meet a deadline while others never miss one.

- What is your relationship to time?
- Are you a planner or a procrastinator?
- Do you tend to arrive on time and expect the same of others? Or . . .
- Do you see time as flexible, appointments as adjustable?
- Are you often the last to arrive at meetings or appointments?

Depending on your time boundaries, you may frequently feel frustrated by someone else's apparent disregard for your time, or you may constantly defend your reasons for running late.

Personal Space

Personal space at work is tricky because it's yours but not yours. You may be assigned to a desk, given a computer, offered office supplies, but each piece of property ultimately belongs to the company. Many people personalize their work areas. Still, company space is not subject to the same rules as personal space at home.

How people relate to personal space in the workplace varies greatly. Some people see all space as "communal." For them, your chair equals my chair; your supplies are my supplies. Others have more strictly defined boundaries. They believe that each person has his or her own physical property, and that "territory" should be respected at all costs. These individuals have rules about how and when their personal space may be used, as well as who may touch or use their belongings.

Personal space includes physical contact. For some touchy-feely people gestures such as hugging, kissing, or putting an arm around someone's shoulder constitute normal interpersonal exchanges at work. Others believe that physical contact at work should not exceed a handshake. They find other forms of physical contact offensive.

- Do you feel comfortable sharing your workspace with others?
- Are there certain personal items that you do not like anyone to touch (telephone, computer, calendar, objects on your desk)?
- How do you feel about physical contact at work?
- Are you uncomfortable when a coworker hugs you?

Depending on your personal space boundaries, you may feel constantly assaulted and angry by individuals who "invade your space," or you may be hurt and confused when colleagues admonish you for mishandling their personal property.

Keeping Your Word

The ability to make and fulfill commitments varies greatly from one person to another. Some people live by the credo "You're as good as your word." These individuals are very careful only to make promises that they are sure they can fulfill. For others, however, commitments have a more fluid quality. These yay-sayers may assert that they will meet certain obligations—like giving you a raise or completing their part of a project—but their delivery falters as the deadline approaches. How do you approach this area of your work life?

- Do you keep your commitments at all costs?
- Do you see commitments as fluid and changeable?
- Have you been the recipient of unfulfilled promises at work?

- Do you sometimes make promises in the excitement of the moment, only to realize you can't deliver?

If you are someone who is very careful about giving your word, then you may assume others operate from the same premise. On the other hand, if you see commitments as adjustable, you may be baffled if a coworker or employee becomes furious when you don't fulfill an earlier promise.

Personal Information

Every workplace is a community of sorts, but not everyone is on the same page regarding how much of their personal life they want to reveal to members of their workplace community. In addition, individuals differ concerning the amount of "delicate" information they want to know about their colleagues.

- How much do you talk about your personal life at work?
- How much do you want to know about your coworkers' personal lives?
- Do you give your colleagues regular updates about your home life, your family, and your love life?
- Do you prefer to keep all aspects of your personal life private?

Depending on your boundaries, you may feel invaded by the "tell-all" coworker's personal narratives, or you may feel snubbed when a coworker doesn't want to hear about your latest escapade.

Emotional Expression

Like it or not, where human interaction takes place, emotions follow. People differ widely in their comfort level when it comes to expressing feelings or fielding the emotional reactions of others. For some, the ability to state when they are angry, upset, or excited about something at work is of vital importance. For these individuals repression of emotional expression is tantamount to oppression.

Others believe that it is more professional to contain feelings. For these individuals, not emoting is a sign of self-mastery and self-control.

- Is it important for you to express your emotions at work?
- Are strong displays of emotion such as crying, yelling, or laughing hysterically acceptable in the workplace?
- Do you prefer to keep your emotions contained and under control?
- Do other people's emotional outbursts make you uncomfortable?

Depending on your boundaries in this area, you may feel assaulted by a coworker or boss who frequently vents his or her feelings in your presence, or you may feel reined in by someone who asks you to be "less emotional" on the job.

Manners/Courtesy

Manners are the social customs practiced in a society or community that show respect to others. What constitutes courteous behavior depends on the individual. One person may make it a point to say "hello" to everyone, open the door for others, and bookend all requests with "Please" and "Thank you." Another person may see greetings as a waste of time, assuming that everyone can fend for themselves, and never bother with "'Please" or "Thank you."

- Are you someone who normally says things like "After you," "Excuse me," and "Thank you"?
- Are those kinds of gestures a waste of your time?
- Do you believe coworkers should greet you with terms like "Good morning," "Hello," or "How are you"?
- Are you offended if someone speaks to you in a brusque tone?

If courtesy and manners are very important to you, a colleague who doesn't share those values will inadvertently cross your boundaries in this area. If manners mean little to you, you may become indignant when a work associate accuses you of discourteous behavior.

Noise

People have different levels of noise sensitivity and noise comfort. Noise at the office can include the volume of speaking voices, music, machinery, or technological devices (phones, cell phones, beepers). Sometimes the personal habits of coworkers such as sneezing, throat clearing, gum chewing, coughing, or constant chattering may invade your space.

- Are you comfortable in a noisy environment?
- Do certain kinds of noise make it difficult for you to concentrate?
- Do you feel energized by loud voices, high-volume music, and boisterous sounds?
- Do you prefer a quiet environment with soft voices, low-volume music, and muted sounds?

If you are someone who is sensitive to noise, you may feel assaulted by the sounds emanating from others. If you are noise tolerant, you may be surprised to discover that sounds such as music playing, cell phones ringing, and loud voices conversing rattle the nerves of your coworkers.

Is Someone Busting Your Boundaries?

We call the people and events that infringe on your personal territory **Boundary Busters**. The coworker who sits near you and talks so loudly that you can't concentrate is a Boundary Buster. A customer who illicitly obtains your home phone number and calls you during the weekend is a Boundary Buster. The boss who intercepts, opens, and reads your mail is a Boundary Buster.

Because their actions invade your personal territory, Boundary Busters can be a source of great emotional and mental distress. The best way to identify a Boundary Buster is to notice your emotional response to their behavior.

If you are continually angry, upset, or complaining about someone or something, you probably need to set a boundary.

This point offers a constructive way to use the negative feelings that someone else's Boundary Busting behavior may trigger in you. Recurring sensations of anger, frustration, irritation, or annoyance often indicate that you are in a situation where someone or something is crossing one of your interpersonal boundaries.

If your coworker's loud conversations infuriate you, that anger informs you of the need to set a noise boundary. If you feel agitated by the customer who illicitly obtains your home phone number, your distress signals the necessity for limits regarding customer access to your personal information. If you feel outraged at the thought of your boss intercepting and reading your mail, that fury can propel you to draw the line regarding anyone intercepting your correspondence.

Once you have identified a person or situation as a Boundary Buster, you can begin the unhooking process.

Unhook physically: Take steps to release tension and calm down your nervous system. Boundary Busters tend to generate a good deal of physical stress.

Unhook mentally: Assess your situation and devise options in terms of setting boundaries.

Unhook verbally: Communicate your interpersonal boundary to the person or people who need to know.

Unhook with a business tool: Take concrete business actions to reinforce the boundary you've just set.

The following scenarios depict real-life situations where individuals were able to respond to Boundary Busting circumstances with unhooking techniques.

Setting a Time Boundary

Clark is an account manager for a small West Coast ad agency. He handles the print ads for his company. Clark has one account that causes him constant agitation. It involves a large seafood restaurant that places daily ads in the local papers. The restaurant's manager, Walter, is responsible for calling these ads in to the agency so that the production department can prepare them for print. The problem is that Walter always waits until 4 p.m. to call in ads he wants placed in the newspapers that same night. Walter's late orders force the agency's production department to stay overtime until 7 or 8 p.m.

Even though Clark asks Walter to call in his requests earlier, and even though Walter always apologizes for his last-minute orders, this pattern continues for six months. With each month, the production department grows increasingly angry with Clark, and Clark becomes increasingly frustrated and upset with Walter. However, because the seafood restaurant is a big account, Clark fears setting any limits with Walter.

Finally, Clark receives a visit from his supervisor regarding the matter. She informs him that the agency can't afford to pay the production department overtime every night for the sake of one late client. Clark nods in agreement, but he still feels anxious about setting a boundary. With his supervisor's guidance, he begins to unhook.

Unhook physically: During his lunch break, Clark goes for a walk just to clear his head.

Unhook mentally: As he walks, he considers his situation:

- What's happening here? *I have an account that's out of control. Walter keeps me and the production department waiting all day, then calls in his ad requests so late that we all work overtime to complete them.*
- What's the client's part? *Walter obviously has trouble managing his time effectively. Even though I ask him to contact us earlier in the day, he keeps waiting until the last minute.*

- What's my part? *I'm not managing the account properly. Other account managers don't seem to have the same problem with their account liaisons. I need to set a time boundary with Walter.*
- What are my options? *Let the situation continue and possibly get fired, or figure out how to solicit better behavior from my client. I can meet with my supervisor to find out what is permissible in terms of laying down rules with our clients.*

Unhook verbally: After meeting with his supervisor, Clark calls Walter and sets a boundary by communicating the following: "The restaurant's business means a great deal to our agency, but we can't properly execute your ads when we receive them so late in the day. In the future, I can't accept any jobs for same-day delivery after 1 p.m. If we do receive them later, I'll have to tack on a rush fee to pay for staff overtime."

Unhook with a business tool: After delivering his message, Clark takes concrete business actions to further manage the account. He sends Walter a memo repeating the new policy and soliciting the restaurant's help in solving the problem. Clark also initiates a monitoring system to help his tardy client meet the new criteria: He calls Walter at 10 a.m. to find out what kinds of print ads he may require that day. He checks in with Walter again at noon, and gives a "final call" at 1 p.m., ready to take Walter's advertising order.

Setting a Personal Space Boundary

We return to Glenda and her spatially invasive coworker, Sam. As Glenda steams outside of her cubicle, she realizes that it's time to set a boundary. After Sam finally extracts himself from her workspace, Glenda begins the process of unhooking.

Unhook physically: Glenda immediately calls to book a massage for that evening to help her release tension and cool down.

Unhook mentally: As she lies on the massage table, Glenda describes her situation to the massage therapist:

- *What's happening here? I have a coworker who is invading my space by usurping my cubicle whenever I leave the building. He eats his lunch, calls his friends, and leaves his debris in my workspace. It's driving me crazy.*
- *What's his part? After obtaining my permission once to make a phone call, Sam assumes it's okay to use my cubicle whenever I am not there.*
- *What's my part? To date, I haven't said anything. I keep ignoring the problem, hoping that he and it will go away.*
- *What are my options? I can continue to get upset and say nothing, I can post a sign outside of my cubicle that reads "KEEP OUT," I can ask my boss to admonish Sam for using my cubicle without my permission, or I can confront Sam myself.*

Unhook verbally: Glenda decides to be brave and approach Sam herself. The next morning, she calls him over to her workspace and conveys the following: "I need to ask you to stop going into my cubicle when I am out of the office. My workspace contains confidential information and I'd like it to be left alone." As Sam nods in understanding, Glenda continues, "I originally said yes to your request because I thought it was a one-time favor. If you have an emergency of some sort you can ask to use my phone. Otherwise, please do not go into my cubicle."

Unhook with a business tool: After their conversation, Glenda shoots Sam a quick e-mail, thanking him for respecting her privacy. She also documents the exchange, just in case Sam "forgets'" the boundary that she just laid down.

Keeping Your Word

Charlie is an up-and-coming superstar for a large sports equipment outlet. He's one of the lead salesmen. Charlie presents himself as a "can-do" kind of guy. He always says yes. When Charlie's boss asks him to give the promotions department a hand during the summer season, he says, "Of course."

Charlie partners up with Bob in promotions. Together, they're supposed to organize a campaign that involves distributing Frisbees imprinted with the store logo at summer concerts and street fairs throughout the region. To begin the planning process, Bob schedules a meeting with Charlie for 4 p.m. on a Monday. Charlie agrees to meet at that time.

By 4:30 p.m. on Monday afternoon, however, Charlie has yet to appear. When Bob calls Charlie on his cell, his colleague apologizes: "I didn't know you meant this Monday. I've got a dentist appointment. Let's meet tomorrow at 5 p.m."

Bob waits another twenty-four hours, only to find himself standing alone at 5 p.m. This time when he calls Charlie, no one answers. The next day, Bob confronts Charlie in the skateboard section of the store. "Where were you? I left messages on your cell and your land line." "Sorry," Charlie says. "I've got a lot on my mind."

Furious with his coworker, Bob walks away. "I'm not wasting my time making another meeting with this guy until I know he'll show up." Bob begins to unhook.

Unhook physically: As soon as he gets home, Bob changes into his cycling gear and goes for a fifteen-mile ride.

Unhook mentally: As he pedals up and down his neighborhood hills, Bob surveys his situation:

- What's happening here? *I'm supposed to be doing a project with a guy who keeps breaking his word. He agrees to meet with me then fails to show.*
- What's Charlie's part? *His mouth says yes but his actions say no.*
- What's my part? *I believed that Charlie meant it when he said he wanted to work on this campaign. Now I'm not so sure.*
- What are my options? *I can go to our manager and complain, or I can deal with Charlie directly.*

Unhook verbally: The next day, Bob walks up to Charlie and states the following: "You said that you wanted to help with this promotions project, but your actions don't match. If you don't want to work on this campaign, say so. Otherwise, the next meeting we set,

I'll expect you to arrive on time. If not, I'll have to report you."

Unhook with a business tool: Following that conversation, Bob documents the two missed meetings and his statement just in case he needs them for future reference.

Setting a Boundary Regarding Personal Information

Jody has been working for Maxine, a reputable theater agent for a large talent agency, for six months. Initially, she felt very excited to assist such a well-known and respected figure within the theater industry. Recently, however, she's begun to question her boss's behavior.

While Jody understands that Maxine's job includes client entertainment, she's surprised at the number of times Maxine returns from her networking lunches with the smell of alcohol on her breath. After these midday social events, Maxine often calls Jody into her office and confesses her darkest secrets. She tells Jody about her deteriorating marriage, her cruel husband, and her waning status in the agency. Jody feels uncomfortable during these conversations, but assumes that she's expected to listen to her boss.

One morning, Maxine intercepts Jody at home just as she's leaving for the office. She implores Jody to cover for her. "My husband thinks I went out of town yesterday on a business trip. If he calls, tell him I'm arriving from Chicago this afternoon. I'll explain the rest to you when I see you."

As Maxine predicts, her husband does call the office that morning. When he asks where his wife is, Jody recites Maxine's fabricated story. While Jody manages to lie successfully, she hangs up the phone feeling dishonest and upset. "Deceiving someone's husband is not in my job description," Jody protests. She begins to unhook.

Unhook physically: Jody goes to the gym during lunch to purge the bad feelings generated from lying for her boss. She swims twenty laps in the gym pool and spends ten minutes in the steam room.

Unhook mentally: As Jody sweats out the toxins, she considers her situation:

- What's happening here? *My new boss Maxine keeps confiding in me. At first it was flattering, but now it includes listening to her after she's been drinking, and lying to her husband.*
- What's Maxine's part? *She's using me as a confidante and accomplice.*
- What's my part? *I'm agreeing to fulfill those roles.*
- What are my options? *I can continue to get deeper into her drama, or I can pull myself out of the play. I can tell Maxine that I'm uncomfortable holding information that could be used against her.*

Unhooking verbally: When Maxine finally returns from her "business trip," Jody walks over to her office and knocks gently on the door. Maxine waves her in. "Thanks for covering for me," she says with a wink. "You're a real pal." Jody closes Maxine's door and states the following: "After this last incident, I realize that it would be best for me not to know any personal information that could get you into trouble. I'm not comfortable lying, so please don't put me in that position again." Maxine is visibly disappointed, but she apologizes for putting Jody in an uncomfortable position.

Unhook with a business tool: As a follow-up to their conversation, Jody e-mails Maxine the following: *"I just want to thank you for our conversation earlier today. I really enjoy working for you and have learned so much over the past six months. I am glad that we can agree to keep our conversations and confidences on a strictly professional level."* After sending the e-mail, Jody further protects herself by putting a word in to HR to be notified of any opportunities for a transfer.

Setting an Emotional Expression Boundary

Beatrice is the receptionist for a busy dental office. She loves her job. She likes interacting with the patients, and she takes pains to remember every patient's name. Beatrice's boss, Dr. Jackson, appreciates his receptionist's enthusiasm but has one major complaint: He feels uncomfortable with her high level of emoting at the office.

Beatrice hugs and kisses longtime patients. She yells at messengers and delivery people when they are late. She cuddles and coos at babies and toddlers. If something strikes Beatrice as funny, she bursts into hysterical laughter. Although she works hard, her effusive style often seems a bit extreme for a dental practice.

One day Mr. Miller, a longtime patient, arrives for his appointment and mentions that his wife recently passed away. Upon hearing the sad news, Beatrice begins to sob so loudly that Dr. Jackson runs into the waiting room. As he attempts to calm his weeping receptionist, the widowed patient, Mr. Miller, looks on in disbelief. A few hours later, Dr. Jackson draws the line. "This has gone too far," he determines. "I've got to make it clear that emotional outbursts are not acceptable in my office." He begins to unhook.

Unhook physically: Dr. Jackson goes home and takes a long run that evening. During the run he thinks about how to handle his valuable yet overly emotive employee.

Unhook mentally: Dr. Jackson takes an inventory of his situation:

- What's happening here? *Beatrice has a hard time filtering or controlling her emotions. Her outbursts make me uncomfortable and create a less professional atmosphere in my office.*
- What's her part? *Beatrice is obviously an emotionally expressive person. She may not be aware of the effect her behavior has on others.*
- What's my part? *To date, I've never told her that I have a problem with her effusive style.*
- What are my options? *I can continue to be irritated and uncomfortable with my employee's behavior, or I can set limits on the level of emotional expression I want in my office.*

Unhook verbally: The next day, Dr. Jackson meets with Beatrice and says, "What happened with Mr. Miller yesterday was inappropriate for a professional dental practice. We have to establish some ground rules for acceptable behavior in this office. From now on, anyone working for me must refrain from emotional outbursts. That includes yelling, crying, and hysterical laughter." Beatrice is hurt and begins tearing. "I know this isn't easy," Dr. Jackson concedes, "but it's important. Please work with me on this."

Unhook with a business tool: After the meeting, Dr. Jackson converts his interpersonal boundary into office policy. He adds a new category to his employee handbook entitled "Professional Behavior and Decorum": "*All employees of this practice agree to speak and communicate in a calm, measured manner, refraining from emotional outbursts of any kind.*" Over the next few weeks, he monitors Beatrice carefully to see whether she's able to conduct herself in accordance with this new rule.

Setting Manners and Courtesy Boundaries

Rhonda and Barb are two nurses who work different shifts on the same oncology unit of a large county hospital. Rhonda oversees the night shift, from 11 p.m. to 7 a.m., and Barb covers the day shift, from 7 a.m. to 3 p.m. Every morning at 6:45 a.m., Barb arrives on the floor and begins taking over for Rhonda.

Barb really enjoys her job, but she can't stand dealing with Rhonda. When she greets Rhonda with a friendly "Good morning," Rhonda doesn't reciprocate. Instead, she grunts and launches into a status report highlighting all of the problematic patients. If Barb helps Rhonda by coming in early or assisting with patient care, Rhonda never says thank you. Whenever Rhonda needs medical supplies of some kind, she never says please, she just orders Barb to restock. "I feel unappreciated," Barb complains. "Rhonda treats me like her personal servant instead of her coworker."

One morning, after Barb says, "Good morning," only to see Rhonda look up and scowl, she realizes that she can't continue working under these conditions. Rhonda's lack of civility is negatively affecting her. Barb needs to set a boundary and see if her coworker can comply. She begins to unhook.

Unhook physically: After work, Barb goes to her yoga class and focuses on releasing tension from her body. As she drives home, she attempts to formulate a constructive approach to Rhonda.

Unhook mentally: Barb takes a mental inventory of the situation:

- What's happening here? *I'm working with someone who has a very different social orientation from mine. Rhonda does not engage in greetings, and gives orders without saying please or thank you.*
- What's Rhonda's part? *Clearly, she doesn't see these simple courtesies as necessary. She may consider them to be a waste of time.*
- What's my part? *I find her behavior offensive. I feel like she's being disrespectful. At the same time, I haven't said anything to her about it yet.*
- What are my options? *I can send Rhonda an anonymous copy of* Miss Manners, *or I can meet with her and tell her how her behavior affects me.*

Unhook verbally: The next time she sees Rhonda, Barb asks for a brief meeting with her. "I know it's not required, but it would make a big difference to me if you would say 'Good morning' when we see each other. I like to hear 'Thank you' when I've done someone a favor, and 'Please' when someone is asking a favor of me. Is that okay with you?"

Unhook with a business tool: Barb can document this conversation with Rhonda—including Rhonda's response. If the situation doesn't improve, Barb may request a transfer and use this interaction as proof of her attempt to improve their professional relationship.

Setting a Noise Boundary

Hank and Brock both work in the customer service division of a major telephone company. They sit in workstations separated by cushioned dividers. The dividers are supposed to absorb some of the sound. In Brock's case, however, nothing absorbs his bellowing voice.

It seems to Hank that Brock literally yells when he speaks with customers. Often, Brock stands up during his conversations, which makes his voice carry like a megaphone. Everything about him is loud. In addition to his thunderous voice, his sneeze sounds like a foghorn. When he laughs, Hank's cubicle vibrates. Even his yawn has a piercing quality.

When Brock is in the office, Hank can barely hear his own conversations with customers. He is often forced to ask them to repeat themselves several times. He has difficulty concentrating on anything other than the sound of his boisterous coworker. At the end of every day, Hank leaves work with a headache.

After months of struggling with Brock's racket, Hank finally meets with their mutual supervisor, Mr. Phelps. He describes the situation and concludes with a plea: "I can't focus with this guy next to me. Is there any way to move me or him?" Mr. Phelps gives Hank an apologetic smile. "Hank, this is a tough situation, but I know you can work it out. Unfortunately, we're a full house, and I can't move either of you at this time."

As Hank walks away from that meeting, he realizes that the only way to improve his situation is to unhook.

Unhook physically: That evening, Hank takes his dog for a long stroll. As he breathes in fresh air and takes in the gentle sounds of his neighborhood, he reviews the issue of Brock.

Unhook mentally: Hank takes a mental inventory of the situation:

- What's happening here? *I'm sitting next to a person who is so loud that I'm having a hard time concentrating. The sounds emanating from Brock's cubicle distract me and hurt my job performance.*
- What's Brock's part? *Brock is a loud guy with a big voice. He doesn't seem to be aware of the impact he has on others.*
- What's my part? *I have yet to really say anything. I keep hoping that someone else will complain or that he'll quit.*

- What are my options? *Continue to request a cubicle change (which will take a while), or approach Brock and ask him to lower his volume.*

Unhook verbally: The next morning, Hank goes directly to Brock and states his case. "I'm having a hard time hearing my customers on the phone. You've got a powerful voice that really carries. Can you speak at a lower volume?" Brock looks surprised. "I'm sorry, man. I didn't realize. I'll try to keep it down. If I get too loud again, let me know."

Unhook with a business tool: Bolstered by his coworker's responsiveness, Hank creates a system for informing Brock when the sound of his voice begins to invade the workplace. Hank constructs a sign that reads, "Lower the volume." Whenever Brock's voice gets too loud, he raises the sign above the divider in Brock's direction.

As you can see from each of these case studies, setting clear interpersonal boundaries at work is a process. You have to identify exactly who or what is encroaching on your personal terrain and assess the options available to you in terms of laying down a limit. Then you have to communicate what you want from the other person or persons in clear, concrete terms. Here are some additional guidelines to setting clear interpersonal boundaries in the workplace:

When setting a limit with someone, state it clearly, without anger, in as few words as possible.

When another person's behavior invades your personal territory, it's often tempting to communicate your discomfort via heated expletives or lengthy explanations. You will be most effective if you keep your boundary statements short, unemotional, and constructive. For example, if you want to set a noise boundary with your boisterous coworker, try to avoid blurting out, "WILL YOU SHUT UP? I CAN'T GET YOUR JABBERING VOICE OUT OF MY

HEAD!" Instead, take yourself through the unhooking process. As you prepare to unhook verbally, craft a simple, factual statement like, "I'm having a hard time concentrating. Please lower your voice."

Also, do not set a boundary until you've cooled off. You'll notice that in all of our scenarios the central characters engaged in some kind of physical activity—walking, running, swimming, or getting a massage—before setting a boundary. They unhooked physically and mentally *first* so that they could address the Boundary Buster from a calmer perspective. Make sure you do the same.

Don't set a boundary unless you're prepared to maintain it.

It's one thing to set a boundary, it's another thing to maintain it once you've put the boundary in place. Like the guards who protect the borders of a country, you must be willing to protect and reinforce any boundary that you set.

Once you put an interpersonal boundary in place, one of several things may happen:

1. Life is beautiful—The person on the receiving end understands and agrees to fulfill your request. You get to enjoy the fruits of your boundary setting immediately.
2. Partial success—The person on the receiving end respects your boundary for a while, but gradually relapses into their old behavior. In this case, you will have to reinforce the border in some way.
3. Continued assault—The person doesn't like or can't respect your boundary and continues to invade your physical, emotional, or psychological territory. In these situations, you'll have to take stronger measures.

Life Is Beautiful

We check in with Clark at the advertising agency a year later. The turmoil he experienced between Walter (his chronically late client) and the production department is now a faded memory. Walter credits his success to the daily calls he makes to Arthur, coupled with Walter's fear of incurring a rush fee if he submits the restaurant's print ads after 1 p.m. Clark's proactive approach to managing his tardy client has allowed Walter to adopt a new way of placing ads within a shorter time frame.

Partial Success

Glenda experiences a more limited victory. After she confronts Sam about using her cubicle, she enjoys two weeks of privacy. One day, however, she returns from lunch to find an empty soda can. It's Sam's brand. She puts the can on his desk with a note that reads, *"See me. Glenda."* Sam manages to avoid Glenda for the next week. A month passes, and the problem seems resolved. One Friday, however, Glenda walks in on Sam once again using her phone. This time, she sets a stronger boundary. "The next time I find you in here without my permission, I'm reporting you." With that, Sam apologizes and does not attempt to cross the line again.

Continued Assault

After Barb communicates her desire to be treated in a more courteous manner by Rhonda, her colleague expresses an opposing point of view. "Look, this is not some cozy sorority, and I am not here to indulge in sweet talk. If you don't like the way I address you, that's too bad." Rhonda doesn't change her conduct at all.

Initially, Barb feels disappointed and hurt by Rhonda's response. Still, she doesn't want to be held hostage by her coworker's negativity. She makes two decisions: First, she decides to practice advanced unhooking (see Chapter 4, "Fatal Attractions"), which includes detaching from Rhonda and depersonalizing her behavior. "I don't have to take her rudeness personally," Barb reminds herself. "And I refuse to let her poor etiquette ruin my day." Second, she takes steps to protect herself. If Rhonda won't change, Barb will. She applies for a transfer to another unit or a different floor.

Wrapping It Up

As these examples illustrate, boundary setting is an ongoing process—not just a one-time thing. In this chapter we've given you seven of the most common areas in which individuals tend to invade each other's personal territory, but the possibilities for boundary infractions are endless. Here are a few other interpersonal zones where you or someone you know may cross a boundary:

- Smells—perfume, body odor, food
- Food—eating other people's food, someone stealing your food, people leaving food around
- Language—foul language, offensive words, off-color jokes
- E-mail—chain letters, distasteful jokes, spam, polls, solicitations
- Cell phones—ringing, interrupting meetings, hearing private conversations in public places
- Personal hygiene—dirty hair, stained clothes, halitosis (bad breath)

In the world of work, boundary setting is one of the most valuable skills you can develop. The more you practice, the better you'll become at identifying and communicating your interpersonal borders to another person. The next time someone invades your physical, emotional, or psychological space, set a boundary. Unhook physically, mentally, verbally, and with a business tool. Then continue to reinforce your new boundary. With every boundary you successfully put into place, you'll experience less frustration and greater satisfaction in the workplace.

THE BUSINESS OF BOUNDARIES AT A GLANCE

Boundary Basics

1. Interpersonal boundaries are invisible. They differ from person to person.
2. You set boundaries by communicating them through your words and actions.
3. Mixed messages yield mixed results.

Time—Be willing to set and maintain time limits.

Personal space—State your rules for the use of your stuff.

Keeping your word—Notice whose actions match their words.

Personal information—Draw the line when you've heard more than you need to know.

Emotional expression—Let others know your comfort zone.

Manners/courtesy—Remember it's okay to ask for the common courtesies you seek.

Noise—Find ways to turn down the volume, or invest in earplugs.

When Setting a Boundary . . .

1. **Unhook physically:** Take steps to release tension and calm down your nervous system. Boundary busters tend to generate a good deal of physical stress.
2. **Unhook mentally:** Assess your situation and devise options in terms of setting limits.
3. **Unhook verbally:** Communicate your interpersonal boundary to the person or people who need to know.
4. **Unhook with a business tool:** Take concrete business actions to reinforce the boundary you've just set.

3

If the Role Fits, You Don't Have to Wear It

HOW TO UNHOOK FROM CONFINING ROLES AT WORK

1. Determine which role you're playing.
2. Choose one characteristic within the role you're willing to change.
3. Practice that new behavior for thirty days.

Josie, a thirty-two-year-old production assistant for a local TV news show, is hooked. No project is too big for her. She's available to work 24/7. She wears three beepers, a pencil in her hair, and a Palm Pilot strapped to her belt. Josie is always there in an emergency. She's a real problem-solver, yet coworkers often avoid her. Recently, Josie has begun to feel tired and resentful. "I haven't been promoted in three years," she complains. "I don't feel recognized for any of the sacrifices I've made." But, instead of demanding better wages or a higher title, what does Josie do? She just works harder.

Although she may not realize it, Josie's problems stem from her own behavior. She's stuck in a role. She's playing the Martyr. For things to get better, *she's* got to change.

Nobody likes to hear this, but sometimes the problem at work is *you*. Without even knowing it, you may be hooked into a role that's killing you at work. Playing a role is like portraying a character in a play. Most of us take on specific roles early in life. They are the way we gain our sense of value in our first group environment—the family.

You can bet that Robin Williams was the Entertainer at his family gatherings. Colin Powell probably played the part of Hero in his early life. Madonna certainly personified a Rebel from the time she could talk back. Whatever roles you enacted as a child, it's likely you'll repeat them at work. A role limits you if . . .

- You feel "branded" or boxed in as a certain kind of person.
- You find that others often misinterpret the intention of your actions.
- You're constantly overlooked or excluded from promotions or raises.

As you read through the following list of roles, you'll probably identify who among your coworkers could be cast in each of these parts. It's easy to see how others act, but more difficult to identify our own tendencies. We challenge you to look for your part.

- **The Hero**—The need to be idolized compels this individual to produce more and perform better than everyone else.
- **The Caretaker**—Feels responsible for and tries to solve everyone else's personal problems.
- **The Rebel/Scapegoat**—Bends the rules and goes against the grain . . . even when it jeopardizes his or her career.
- **The Martyr**—Wants recognition and praise for sacrifice and suffering on behalf of the company.
- **The Entertainer**—Uses jokes and humor to break the tension and keep others happy.
- **The Peacemaker**—Does whatever it takes to keep the peace.
- **The Invisible One**—Stays out of trouble by staying out of the spotlight.

There are two sides to any role:

1. Taking on the part—Unconsciously enacting a certain set of behaviors.
2. Becoming "branded" as a certain kind of person—This occurs when the people at work only see you through a specific lens. For example, no matter how many good deeds a Rebel does, coworkers may only see that person's unruly side.

Playing a specific role at work becomes a hook if, like Josie, it constricts you professionally or limits your ability to move ahead.

Before you can unhook from a role, you must first be able to identify that you're playing it. Many people play roles they aren't even aware of. For instance, if you're always trying to break tension between coworkers by telling jokes, if you feel you have to charm and amuse all of your colleagues, and if you have trouble confronting people directly when something bothers you, you may be trapped in the position of workplace Entertainer.

On the other hand, if you feel compelled to shock your coworkers by making provocative statements, if your "independent spirit" hampers your ability to be part of any team, and if you constantly clash with people in positions of authority, your role as office Rebel may be holding you back. In some cases, an individual may take on several roles in the workplace. What's important is to determine which role(s) you're playing and how it may be limiting your ability to thrive at work.

The Hero

This individual is the superhuman of the workplace. A Hero takes great pride in solving any problem that crosses his or her path. Every Hero is naturally resourceful and wise beyond his or her years. These individuals see themselves as capable and competent in any situation. Their consistent high energy and can-do attitude make them invaluable to any work situation. New employees often think that the Hero owns the company.

It's great to be a Hero until it limits you. You're hooked into the Hero role if you can never say no, and you take on more responsibility than is humanly possible. Heroes can overwork themselves to the point of jeopardizing their health or ruining their home life.

Read the following questions and put a check by the statements that accurately describe your behavior:

_____ Are you generally the first one to arrive at work and the last one to leave?

_____ Have you given up or canceled your vacations because of work?

_____ Do you insist on doing business during off-hours?

_____ Are you constantly asked to solve problems that aren't in your job description?

_____ Do you have a problem saying no whenever someone asks you to take on another responsibility?

The Caretaker

Caretakers are the natural counselors of the workplace. They have a gift for listening, for making people feel comfortable and safe. They will ask you questions about your home life, and before you know it, you're confiding in them. Caretakers enjoy solving other people's personal problems. Their ability to provide emotional support for others makes them feel valuable.

It's fine to be a Caretaker until it impairs you. You're hooked into a Caretaker role if your knowledge of an individual's personal problems prevents you from holding that person accountable at work. If you suspect that you're a Caretaker, read the following questions and put a check by the statements that accurately describe your behavior:

_____ Are you someone who naturally finds out about your colleagues' private lives?

_____ Do coworkers always divulge their personal problems to you?

_____ Do you make excuses for people at work based on your knowledge of their personal issues?

_____ Do you lower your expectations and compensate for under-functioning employees?

_____ Do you often feel responsible for solving other people's personal problems at work?

The Rebel

Rebels are the nonconformists of the workplace. Naturally independent thinkers, they question all rules, regulations, systems, and conventional ways of doing things. Rebels want to shake things up. A Rebel can be extremely valuable when a company needs to update its standard practices. Because they think in radical ways, Rebels can force other members of a work team to expand their point of view. Generally speaking, Rebels have a hard time trusting people in positions of authority. For this reason, they are often most successful in leadership positions.

It's exciting to be a Rebel until it confines you. You're hooked into the Rebel role if your need to buck the system alienates you from others. Once you're branded as a "troublemaker," coworkers may start avoiding you, and your boss may become increasingly impatient with your need to challenge everyone else's decisions. Some Rebels become the company scapegoat—the person blamed when things go wrong.

If you suspect you may be a Rebel, read the following questions and put a check by the statements that accurately describe your behavior:

_____ Do think of yourself as an independent thinker?

_____ Do you enjoy shocking your coworkers with provocative statements?

_____ In a group situation, do you often take a contrary point of view?

_____ Does getting into a heated argument energize you?

_____ Do you frequently clash with people in positions of authority?

The Martyr

Martyrs are the professional sufferers of the workplace. They sacrifice their time and energy for the sake of the company. While the Hero wants to be recognized for his or her heroic deeds, the Martyr wants to be appreciated for all that he or she gives to the company. Martyrs are very dedicated and hardworking employees. No job is too menial or too dirty for them. If they see a need, they rush in to fill it. For this reason, most Martyrs are extremely busy. All they ask is to be valued and respected for their efforts.

It can be fulfilling to be a Martyr unless it totally drains you. You are hooked into the Martyr role if you feel tired, resentful, and unrecognized for the sacrifices you've made. If you have a sneaking suspicion that you could be a Martyr, read the following questions and put a check by the statements that accurately describe your behavior:

_____ Is your workload bigger than anybody else's?

_____ Do you find yourself rushing in to "save the day" on a regular basis?

_____ Do you secretly feel jealous when a coworker receives positive attention?

_____ Do you feel underappreciated for all that you do?

_____ Do you feel overburdened, overwhelmed, and physically exhausted most of the time?

The Entertainer

Entertainers are the crowd-pleasers of the workplace. An Entertainer knows how to find the humor in any situation and bring it out.

Entertainers can make the most serious and stern employees laugh. They send out funny e-mails, insert jokes at tense meetings, and engage in playful antics with their coworkers. Because they provide so much comic relief, they tend to be quite popular.

It's fun to be an Entertainer until it hampers you. You are hooked into the Entertainer role if your reputation for being a clown prevents others from taking you seriously. Many Entertainers suffer because their ideas and opinions are marginalized. Even when they have something important to say, it's interpreted as a joke.

If you think you could be an Entertainer, read the following questions and put a check by the statements that accurately describe your behavior:

_____ Is your first impulse in any situation to find the humor?

_____ Do you have a knack for making people laugh?

_____ Do you take pride in charming and amusing your coworkers?

_____ Does interpersonal conflict make you uncomfortable?

_____ Do you sometimes wish people took you more seriously?

The Peacemaker

Peacemakers are the diplomats of the workplace. They want everyone to get along. Harmonious by nature, these individuals dislike angry confrontations and unpleasant interactions at work. If two coworkers have a disagreement, the Peacemaker will try to find the common ground. Peacemakers are highly skilled team players who tend to see the positive in everyone. Because they are so easy to get along with, these individuals are usually very well liked.

It's gratifying to be a Peacemaker unless it paralyzes you. You're hooked into a Peacemaker role if your need to keep the peace prevents you from voicing your true opinions and taking a stand. Fear of soliciting disapproval or anger from others can paralyze a Peacemaker, preventing him or her from taking decisive action when it's most needed. Peacemakers can be perceived as wishy-washy because they're so afraid of offending others.

If you identify with the qualities of these workplace mediators, read the following questions and put a check by the statements that describe your behavior:

_____ Are you someone who naturally mediates conflicts between others?

_____ Are you able to find an agreeable point of view between two differing perspectives?

_____ Does the thought of upsetting your coworkers make you anxious?

_____ Do you have a hard time understanding why anyone would want to pick a fight?

_____ Do you have difficulty advocating your point of view at meetings?

The Invisible One

These are the unseen employees of the workplace. Quiet and reserved by nature, Invisible Ones require little or no attention from others. They know how to keep their heads down and their lips sealed. They complete their own work assignments with minimal fanfare. Most people don't see them arrive or leave. Invisible Ones may attend a meeting, a conference, a party, and no one will remember their presence.

It's safe to be invisible until it harms you. If you're too invisible, your finest accomplishments and brightest ideas may go completely unnoticed. You may be perceived as aloof, uncaring, or unfriendly.

If you have a hunch that you may be invisible at work, read the following questions and put a check by the statements that accurately describe your behavior:

_____ Do you prefer to stay out of the limelight?

_____ Do you keep your ideas and opinions to yourself?

_____ Do you take pride in doing your work and "staying out of the way"?

_____ At meetings, do you tend to sit back and observe?

_____ Do you feel that your accomplishments are often ignored or disregarded?

Now that you've surveyed the various roles, you may have an idea of the part(s) that you most frequently play. Remember that no role is problematic unless it limits you professionally or personally. Should you suspect that you *are* trapped in one of these character types, you can unhook by taking the following steps:

1. Decide which role you're playing.
2. Choose one characteristic within that role that you're willing to change.
3. Practice the new behavior for thirty days.

To illustrate this technique, we'll present one case study from each role, and demonstrate how that person learned to unhook.

The Hero

Dominick is the senior artistic director for a major advertising firm. Everybody loves him. He's the first one there and the last one to leave. Dominick doesn't appear to need vacation or sick days. He works long hours and produces amazing campaigns. If you want someone to handle a difficult client, if your computer breaks down, or if you just need a few bucks until payday, go to Dominick. He's the guy who's called into every meeting for his valued opinion. Newcomers to the company think that he owns it.

There's only one problem. Dominick's late hours and heroic actions at work are taking a toll on his home life. His wife keeps threatening to leave if he doesn't spend more time with her. She's furious that he's canceled nine out of ten of their planned vacations. "Even when you do come home," she complains, "you spend hours answering e-mails on your BlackBerry."

After each of these heated conversations, Dominick promises to modify his work habits. For a while, he improves. He makes a concerted effort to leave work in time for the two of them to share dinner. Eventually, however, he returns to his old heroic ways.

Finally, Dominick returns to his house after a long day at the office to find a handwritten note neatly tacked onto the front door: "Gone to find a man who wants to be with me." Dominick is stunned. He never imagined that his demure wife would have the nerve to walk out on him. In the weeks that follow, he begins to seriously examine his behavior. He realizes that he's trapped in a role at work that may be good for his professional reputation, but leaves him with nothing at home.

How Heroes Unhook

The key to breaking free from the Hero role is learning to say no. Heroes like being courageous and accomplishing great things. Their gallantry throws their lives off balance, however, when they can't admit to having human limitations. Deep down, most Heroes dread disappointing anyone. This fear of letting others down or causing displeasure becomes a noose around the Hero's neck. A Hero must understand that he or she can be just as effective and probably more respected by setting limits at work. Here are some options:

1. Refrain from solving any problems that are not within your job description.
2. Leave work at a reasonable hour—6 p.m., rather than 9 or 10.
3. Book and take a vacation.
4. Stop doing business during off-hours.
5. Say no the next time you're asked to take on yet another responsibility. Trust that someone else can rise to the occasion.

Dominick decides to begin unhooking by practicing option two: leaving the office at a reasonable hour (6 p.m. rather than 9 or 10 p.m.). Once home, he also applies behavior number four: He refrains from conducting business outside of the office. At first, breaking the habit of staying late poses a serious challenge. His colleagues poke fun at him for "going soft," and he feels guilty for cutting out so early.

Coworkers challenge Dominick's resolve by approaching him with last-minute problems at 5:45 p.m.—just as he's preparing to leave. Although it's difficult for him to say, "I'll get to this tomorrow," he does manage to spit it out. Over time, he learns that very few items actually require his immediate attention. Meanwhile, Dominick's colleagues realize that their "hero" is not a twenty-four-hour convenience store. They eventually respect the fact that he goes home at a reasonable hour.

To his surprise, Dominick's ability to establish boundaries between the workplace and his home life results in much greater efficiency at work. He becomes more focused and productive. Whenever he's handed a brief, a memo, or any document that needs his attention, he scans it immediately for relevant information. These same documents used to be stuffed into his briefcase and taken home as night reading.

As Dominick develops the ability to set boundaries between himself and his company, he's able to build a life outside of the office. He returns to working out, playing golf, and joining his buddies for Monday night poker. His wife even agrees to date him again. Jumping into the Hero role will always be tempting for Dominick. With practice, he can become more selective about when and where to apply his courageous energy.

The Caregiver

Christine manages a well-established day spa located in the center of a resort town. Her receptionist, Bibi, has been working at the spa for several months. As Christine knows all too well, Bibi has many personal problems. She often calls Christine at the beginning of a workday with the news that her car has broken down. She also seems susceptible to many illnesses. In just six months, she's contracted the flu, two colds, bronchitis, and strep throat. To make matters worse, Bibi's boyfriend recently developed a mysterious neurological disorder. He's unable to work. As the sole breadwinner, Bibi never has enough money. She and her family are in a state of constant crisis.

The more Bibi confides in Christine regarding her personal problems, the more responsible Christine feels for Bibi's welfare. Even though Christine could easily hire a receptionist with fewer difficulties, she keeps Bibi on. "Bibi is a good person who just needs someone to understand and support her," Christine tells herself. "She just needs a break." Christine sincerely believes that responding to Bibi's constant calamities with kindness and compassion will eventually produce better attendance and job performance from her employee.

Meanwhile, other members of the staff resent Bibi because she receives preferential treatment. They can't believe that this chaotic receptionist continues to hold a job. Even when Bibi does grace the spa with her presence, she makes numerous scheduling errors, fails to collect payment from clients, and often forgets to inform staff when their clients have arrived.

One morning, Bibi's car breaks down for the twentieth time. Christine finds herself covering the front desk. A regular massage client walks in, sees Christine, and sighs with relief. "Thank God it's you and not Bibi. Last time I was here, she kept me and several other people waiting for forty-five minutes while she handled some family crisis." In that moment, Christine awakens to the fact that protecting Bibi is hurting business. The desire to rescue this troubled employee is interfering with the spa's ability to service its customers.

How Caretakers Unhook

The key to letting go of the Caretaker role is to become less personal and more professional. A Caretaker needs to focus more on the facts and less on the feelings of any workplace situation. Instead of seeing yourself as a parent or counselor to your colleagues, remember that you are simply a worker among workers. Understand that your tendency to coddle underfunctioning employees doesn't help them. In fact, it keeps them stuck. Use your compassionate nature to practice "tough love." That is, allow each person to be responsible for his or her own actions. Here are some options:

1. STOP having conversations with coworkers about their personal lives.
2. Do not allow coworkers and employees to divulge detailed accounts of their private lives to you. Cut those conversations short with simple statements like "We'd better get to work now."
3. Stop making excuses for people at work based on their personal issues.
4 Refrain from covering up for underfunctioning coworkers
5. Return to your job description; unless you are assigned as a certified social worker to your coworkers, stop shouldering problems and start measuring performance—theirs and yours.

Christine decides to start unhooking from the Caretaker role by practicing number five. Instead of shouldering Bibi's problems, she begins to measure Bibi's performance. She commits to tracking Bibi's attendance for thirty days. After just two weeks, she is shocked by the results. Over the course of two forty-hour workweeks, Bibi arrives late seven out of ten mornings, and puts in less than twenty-five hours per week at the front desk.

Confronted with these facts, Christine understands why every employee at the spa rails against Bibi. She informs her receptionist that her attendance must improve if she wants to keep her job. "From now on, I expect full-time hours for full-time pay." Bibi agrees. "Of course, Christine. I won't let anything get in the way. You're such a good friend. You can count on me."

The next morning, Christine arrives at work to an empty reception desk and a desperate message from Bibi: Her boyfriend stole her car. She can't afford a cab so she won't be in that day. Christine laments that she can no longer make excuses for her troubled receptionist. She calls Bibi at home and lets her go.

The Rebel

Cliff works as an on-air news, weather, and traffic reporter for a local radio station. For the past ten years, he's built a following of early-morning listeners who tune in to hear the "Renegade

Reporter." As Cliff likes to say, "I shock and amuse when I deliver the news."

In an attempt to improve its overall ratings, the station takes on Richard, a new producer. This innovative leader meets with his newly acquired staff and announces his plan to take the station from number three to number one. He informs his crew that he welcomes honest feedback at all times. Richard has an open-door policy and wants to hear from everyone on the team.

Later that day, Cliff makes his way to Richard's office, walks in, and begins to broadcast his views. "I'm so glad you're here. I want to address your goal of making this station number one. You should know that we have a huge hurdle ahead of us." "Why is that?" Richard asks. "Because the number one local station is killing us right now," Cliff says. "I told your predecessor that unless we have better equipment and more resources we don't have a prayer."

Richard looks visibly distressed. He stands up, rubs the back of his neck as if trying to release tension, and walks toward Cliff. "With that kind of attitude, maybe you'd be happier working for the competition," he suggests. Cliff starts to backpedal: "No, that's not what I meant . . ." But by now, Richard has his hand on Cliff's back. "Nice talking to you." He escorts Cliff out of his office and closes the door.

Cliff stands outside of Richard's office feeling dismissed and confused. This is not the first time his candor has been met with resistance. "I was just trying to give the guy some constructive criticism. I don't understand why people always take my ideas the wrong way." While Cliff can easily find fault with Richard's defensive reaction to his remarks, he'd also like to know how to voice his opinion without landing in the penalty box.

How Rebels Unhook

If you want to unhook from the Rebel role, you must be willing to temper your feedback. This does not mean that you have to withhold your opinions. It does mean that you practice packaging your ideas so that others can hear them without feeling offended or attacked. Rebels often feel misunderstood at work because their attempts to express their opinions generate defensive responses from others. Look for ways to deliver your contrary opinions with less shock and more diplomacy. You'll be amazed at the results. Here are some options:

1. Practice impulse control—think before you speak. Before stating your opinion, write down your thoughts.
2. Find a friend who can serve as your editor. When you write a "strong" memo or e-mail, let that person read it *before* you send it out.
3. In group situations (meetings, conference calls), before you express a contradictory point of view, ask your colleagues if they're interested in hearing it.
4. When people in authority make decisions that you don't agree with, take twenty-four hours to ask yourself the following questions:

   • Who owns the company?
   • Who signs my paycheck?
   • Is this decision something I can't live with?
   • Is this a decision I can live with even though I don't agree with it?

5. If you think that your words have offended someone, they probably have. Consider saying, "I'm sorry if my words offended you."

Cliff looks at his options and chooses to practice number one, impulse control. For thirty days, he agrees to write down his thoughts before expressing them to coworkers. At first, he can't see how any of his statements could possibly be modified. "If they don't like what I have to say, that's their problem," he tells himself. But, deep down, he'd really like to master the skill of making a salient point without alienating everyone in the room. He decides to incorporate option two—find a friend who can serve as his editor.

Cliff seeks out the counsel of the most diplomatic person he knows, his sister. She's eager to help him express his opinions in a way that colleagues can tolerate and digest. Cliff e-mails his comments to her, she repackages them, and he delivers the tailored message. Within a few weeks, Cliff begins to experience a different response to his comments at work. He sees that it's possible to be effective and tactful at the same time.

Cliff maintains his ability to "shock and amuse when delivering the news." Off-air, however, he focuses on offering ideas and suggestions that challenge outmoded business practices without offending his coworkers. Richard, the producer, learns to appreciate Cliff's honest approach to building the station's ratings.

The Martyr

For this role, we return to Josie's situation at the local television news show. Josie reads each question and nods a tired yes. Her workload is bigger than anybody else's. She does find herself "saving the day" on a regular basis. She constantly complains to her husband about how little her efforts at work are appreciated. And, while she hates to admit it, she does feel jealous when one of her colleagues receives applause or credit for a job well done. Josie sighs heavily, showing her exhaustion and frustration at being hooked into this role. "But how do I get out of this?" she asks.

How Martyrs Unhook

To break out of the Martyr role, you must be willing to trade in suffering for self-care. This change in orientation can be very frightening because many Martyrs believe that they are only valued for their ability to make sacrifices. The truth is that the sooner you learn to take care of yourself, set limits at work, and ask for what you want, the sooner you'll receive the respect and admiration you crave. Here are some of your options:

1. Reduce your workload. Avoid taking on any additional projects or doing big favors.
2. Delegate tasks to others and give them credit for a job well done.

3. When you're not at work, turn off all communication devices that keep you hooked into the office—beepers, cell phones, e-mail, and voice mail. You'll see that the office can survive without you.

4. Rather than suffer in silence, learn to ask for what you want. If you think you deserve a raise, speak with your supervisor. If you want a promotion, document your performance and request it.

5. Track the number of hours you work and reduce the total by 15 percent. For example, if you work seventy hours a week, reduce to sixty.

Josie decides to start with option one, reducing her workload. For thirty days, she agrees not to take on any additional projects. If someone asks for a favor, she puts option two into action by finding someone else to perform the task. Anytime a special project lands in her lap, she farms it out to her coworkers.

Initially, saying no and passing work on to others fills Josie with anxiety. "What if no one really needs me here?" She worries. Josie also knows that certain coworkers won't like it when she sets limits on of the amount of work she's willing to do. These individuals constantly test her resolve by asking her to "save them" in one way or another.

Over time, however, Josie's new behavior positions her as a leader and manager rather than a suffering Martyr. This improved status among her coworkers inspires her to adjust other aspects of her Martyr conduct at work.

The Entertainer

Mitch is a thirty-two-year-old construction contractor. The youngest son of a large Irish family, he has a gift for being funny, charming, and entertaining in almost any situation. These traits are great when he's meeting a client or trying to convince a subcontractor to work with him. But problems arise when he begins to manage a construction job.

While Mitch knows how to make people laugh, he has a hard time asserting himself or making demands of others. When subcon-

tractors show up late or make mistakes on the job, he doesn't con-front them. Instead, he makes a joke and hopes that they'll behave better next time. Mitch has had a hard time collecting money from his clients. He'll let a customer delay paying him for months.

Recently, Mitch's fear of confrontation and need to be funny have been endangering the financial health of his business. On one end, he's losing money due to the unfinished work of unreli-able subcontractors. On the other end, he's owed thousands of dollars from clients who are slow to pay.

How Entertainers Unhook

Unhooking from the Entertainer role begins with trusting that you have value whether you make people laugh or not. Entertainers need to balance their desire to amuse and keep people happy with a commitment to being respected. This doesn't mean that you can no longer use humor to win people over. It does mean that you develop the concurrent ability to speak, listen, and conduct important busi-ness without clowning around. If you want others to take you more seriously, you must demonstrate that you can be serious when it counts. Here are some options:

1. Try taking a more serious approach to your own career. List the specifics of what you want to accomplish and focus on creating those results rather than humoring your coworkers.
2. In tense moments, when you feel the urge to insert a joke, prac-tice saying nothing.
3. If you want something from someone, practice asking for it directly without making a joke or an apology.
4. Be willing to set limits with people whose behavior angers you.
5. Be willing to trade in popularity for respect.

Mitch surveys his options and settles on number three—asking for what he wants directly without making a joke or an apology. He begins with one of his clients, Mr. Fallon, who repeatedly fails to pay on time. At this point, Mitch and his subcontractors are owed over $25,000. Mitch feels justified about insisting on payment. At the same time, he fears angering this customer.

For two days, Mitch rehearses his statement in front of the bathroom mirror. "My crew and I can no longer afford to work on your job without payment. If you'd like us to continue renovating your home, I need payment in full for the last invoice. Once I receive the check, we'll get back to work."

The next morning, Mitch finds Mr. Fallon at home. He approaches him, shakes his hand, and smiles. For the first time, he refrains from making a funny remark to ease the tension. Instead, he delivers his prepared speech. After getting the words out, Mitch braces for Mr. Fallon's negative reaction. He prepares for a heated argument. To his surprise, Fallon doesn't put up a fight. "Thanks for reminding me, Mitch. You usually seem so relaxed about payment that it often slips my mind. In the future, please bring this to my attention sooner."

For the next four weeks, Mitch continues to apply option three to his conversations with subcontractors, architects, and clients. He continues to be charming and amiable to everyone he meets. But when he needs to address a tough topic like money, contracts, productivity, or deadlines, Mitch does his best to keep it simple and state what he wants. To his surprise, most of his business relationships show a marked improvement. People seem to appreciate it when he clearly spells out his expectations. The individuals who cannot meet him halfway disqualify themselves from any future business dealings.

The Peacemaker

Cindy works as the daytime manager for a large drugstore. She oversees a staff of eight. Two of her employees, Anthony and Rita, constantly bicker with each other. They disagree about everything. They argue about the correct price of an item while customers are waiting at the register; they quarrel over how to catalog the merchandise while they're taking inventory; they even squabble about whose turn it is to go on break.

Cindy hears them bickering and it really bothers her. At first, she tries to intervene. She walks up to them while they're

*embroiled in a yet another heated dispute: "Come on, you guys,"
she says. "You know this isn't productive. Let's get back to work."
For a moment, they stop fighting. Twenty minutes later, however,
Anthony and Rita are at it again.*

*One day the owner of the store spontaneously drops in while
Cindy is at lunch. He finds her two quarrelsome coworkers fighting
over how to operate the credit card machine while three frustrated
customers stand in line. He becomes furious, and reprimands
Cindy. "If you can't control your employees, you're not qualified to
manage this store." Cindy has two weeks to improve the situation,
or all three of them are fired.*

How Peacemakers Unhook

Unhooking from the Peacemaker role requires two fundamental
adjustments: (1) a willingness to be disliked in the short run; (2) an
ability to tolerate situations that are emotionally uncomfortable.
Peacemakers assume that angry confrontations and tense interactions only produce negative results. For this reason, they fear and
avoid anything that might generate angry feelings in another
human being.

Unfortunately, many situations in business require confrontations of one kind or another. For example, unruly employees must
be addressed and admonished for their behavior. A Peacemaker will
experience immense freedom if he or she can trust that short-term
emotional discomfort often produces long-term positive change.
Here are some options:

1. To reduce your fear of displeasing others, practice saying no,
   even if it's to yourself.
2. When conflicts arise, don't jump in to arbitrate. Insist that the
   individuals involved work out their differences without you
   playing mediator.
3. Find ways to express your point of view clearly, with as little
   hedging as possible. Avoid phrases like "kind of," "sort of,"
   "maybe," "possibly," "it would be nice if . . ." These statements
   water down your message and weaken your delivery.

4. If someone expresses anger at work, try leaving that person alone rather than attempting to fix it.
5. If you are in a management or supervisory position, practice clearly stating your expectations of others, even when you fear they'll resent you for it.

Cindy knows that if she wants to retain her job as a manager she must implement option five—clearly stating her expectations of others. Like any good Peacemaker, she fears that if she confronts Anthony and Rita, they will never forgive her. Still, she prefers the possibility of generating hard feelings over the certainty of losing her job.

The next time Cindy catches Rita and Anthony bickering she calls them into her small office. "You two have to stop arguing or you can both find another place to work." While she's tempted to soften her remarks so as not to offend her employees, Cindy resists the urge to "make peace." "The next time I catch you bickering," she warns, "one of you is going home, and the other one will have to carry a double workload."

Rita and Anthony are dumbfounded. For three days, they behave perfectly. Then, on a busy Friday afternoon, Cindy finds the quarreling coworkers at it again. This time, she states her expectations even more clearly. "Anthony, please go home for the day. I'll deduct the pay for your early departure. Rita, now you have to carry Anthony's weight in terms of servicing these customers."

Since that incident, Anthony and Rita have stopped fighting in public. On occasion, Cindy may hear them begin to bait each other. At those times, she clears her throat and says, "You know the rule . . ." Eventually, Rita and Anthony are able to work side by side without locking horns.

The Invisible One

For fifteen years, Benjamin has quietly performed his duties as the senior botanist for a large urban nature conservancy. His job entails monitoring and tending all rare plants at the conservancy's prominent botanical garden. In a few months, the conservancy plans to launch a new program. This program involves harvest-

ing hydroponic plants. Benjamin is fascinated by the emerging science of hydroponics. He'd like to head up the new division.

For three months, Benjamin regularly slips articles about "tank farming" under the director's door. Each article has a note attached reading, "Thought this might be something for us to pursue." Benjamin assumes that these articles demonstrate his interest in the program.

One Friday, Benjamin arrives at work only to learn that his boastful coworker Trista has been appointed managing director of the hydroponics division. He is shocked and disappointed. "I can't believe this," he says under his breath. "I thought my boss knew that I wanted to launch that program." Suddenly, Benjamin's low-key approach is causing him high anxiety.

How Invisible Employees Unhook

To break out of this hidden role, you must be willing to be seen. Invisible employees often feel safer out of the limelight. They fear making waves because they fear receiving negative attention. A person comfortable with being invisible needs to understand that his or her ideas, opinions, observations, and personal goals *are* important and valuable. You cannot be recognized for your contributions, however, unless they and you are visible to others. Here are some options:

1. Attend meetings, go to conferences, and get involved in the areas that are of greatest interest to you.
2. Begin to state your ideas and opinions to coworkers and managers so that your voice is heard. (When you do say something, make sure that everyone hears you.)
3. Practice speaking up. At meetings, be sure that you have spoken up at least once.
4. Be willing to report your accomplishments. Send out an e-mail, circulate a memo, document your successes in some way.
5. If you want something like a raise or a promotion, don't wait for it to be handed to you. Go and ask for it.

Benjamin discusses his predicament with a good friend and asks for any ideas regarding how he can salvage his situation. The friend recommends he try a revised version of option number five—if you want to work on the hydroponics program, don't wait for it to be handed to you. Go and ask for it.

Benjamin decides that, while he can't change what's already transpired, he can make it clear that he wants to be involved in this exciting initiative. He spends the next week preparing for a meeting with the director. He drafts a document that lists his accomplishments at the botanical gardens and describes the research he's already conducted regarding hydroponics. He lays out his ideas for the conservancy's hydroponics program as well as sources where the conservancy may be able to obtain additional funding.

Benjamin delivers this document to the director, who is noticeably impressed. "I understand that you've assigned Trista to manage our new division," Benjamin explains, "but I'd like to be considered for a position as the department grows. In the meantime, I'd like to participate in any way I can to further this exciting initiative." The director smiles and responds, "I wish you'd come to me a month ago. This is the first time you've spoken to me about any of this. Why don't you and I meet every quarter to discuss possible promotion opportunities? At the same time, you should sit in on the planning committee for our hydroponics program."

For the next month, Benjamin exercises option one—he attends every meeting of the hydroponics planning committee. At these gatherings, he makes a concerted effort to voice his ideas and communicate his expertise in a helpful manner. In between meetings, he keeps his committee members informed by distributing news clippings describing new developments in the field.

As these cases illustrate, breaking out of a role doesn't happen overnight. It takes a concentrated effort to change established patterns of behavior. Coworkers will initially try to pull you back into acting like your "old self." Don't let that deter you. Commit to changing just one aspect of your behavior for thirty days, and you'll reap the benefits of unhooking from any role that keeps you stuck.

IF THE ROLE FITS, YOU DON'T HAVE TO WEAR IT AT A GLANCE

The Hero—the superhuman of the workplace
Unhooking actions:

1. Do not take on additional responsibilities that are not part of your job description.
2. Leave work at a reasonable hour.
3. Take at least one vacation a year.
4. Do not take work home.
5. Do not take on work that would compromise numbers 1–4.

The Caregiver—the natural counselor of the workplace
Unhooking actions:

1. Keep conversations with coworkers about their personal lives to a minimum.
2. Do not let coworkers confide personal details of their lives to you.
3. Stop making excuses for others based on their personal issues.
4. Return to your job description—refrain from acting as an unpaid therapist.
5. Instead of shouldering problems, start measuring the performance of others.

The Rebel—the nonconformist of the workplace
Unhooking actions:

1. Practice impulse control; think before you speak.
2. When sending a written document, find a person to serve as your editor.
3. Before expressing a contrary point of view, ask others if they want to hear it.
4. When authorities make decisions you dislike, take twenty-four hours to think before you speak.
5. When you think you've offended someone, say you're sorry.

The Martyr—the professional sufferer of the workplace
Unhooking actions:

1. Reduce your workload. Don't take on extra projects or special favors.
2. Delegate tasks to others and give them credit for a job well done.
3. When at home, cut off all communication devices—the office will survive without you.
4. Don't suffer in silence. Ask for what you want.
5. Limit the number of hours you work.

The Entertainer—the crowd-pleaser of the workplace
Unhooking actions:

1. Set goals for your career and focus on creating results.
2. In tense moments when you want to insert a joke, practice doing nothing.
3. If you want something, ask for it directly without apologizing or making a joke.
4. Set limits with people whose behavior angers you (see chapter 2, "The Business of Boundaries").
5. Trade in popularity for respect.

The Peacemaker—the diplomat of the workplace
Unhooking actions:

1. Practice saying NO.
2. State what you want even if others won't like you for it.
3. When conflicts arise that don't involve you, avoid jumping in to mediate.
4. Express your point of view clearly without hedging.
5. When a coworker is upset at work, don't try to fix it.

The Invisible One—the unseen employee
Unhooking actions:

1. Be seen—attend meetings, conferences, etc.
2. Be willing to state your ideas and opinions to coworkers.
3. Speak up. At meetings be sure to speak up at least once.
4. Report your accomplishments to coworkers and supervisors.
5. Ask for raises and promotions. Do not wait for them to be handed to you.

4

Haven't We Met Before?
Fatal Attractions at Work

FIVE MOST COMMON BRANDS OF FATAL ATTRACTIONS

- **The Exploder**—Starts out as dynamic; turns into dynamite.
- **The Empty Pit**—Starts out as very nice; turns into very needy.
- **The Saboteur**—Starts out as sweet talk; turns into sabotage.
- **The Pedestal Smasher**—Starts out as fawning; turns into fault-finding.
- **The Chip on the Shoulder**—Starts out as appreciative; turns into argumentative.

You are now entering the advanced zone for unhooking. In this chapter, you'll learn about a more complex kind of relationship. We'll introduce you to the five most common brands of Fatal Attractions at work, as well as the seven stages of these difficult associations. We'll show you another method for unhooking. Should you determine that you are in the grips of a Fatal Attraction, we suggest you pay specific attention to each stage and try to identify where you are.

Fasten your seat belt. The material in this chapter may take you only an hour to read, but your ability to break free from the ties of a Fatal Attraction will require practice, focus, and commitment. You are building new interpersonal muscles, and you'll need patience and perseverance to develop them. We recommend that you study this chapter as many times as it takes to absorb and utilize the material.

Mark is a forty-year-old chief administrator for a pharmaceutical drug company. On this Monday morning, he wakes up with a sick feeling in his stomach. For reasons he can't explain, he dreads going to work. "I just got promoted. I should be happy. Instead, I feel nauseous."

Mark drags himself out of bed and hurries off to work. Once at the office, he launches into his usual routine. He checks in on his staff, returns phone calls, and responds to e-mail. He starts to feel better. "Maybe this will be a decent day after all," he hopes. Then Mark's boss, Mr. Russ, calls him in for an unscheduled meeting.

These "emergency meetings" aren't uncommon for Mr. Russ. Usually, they're yelling sessions that are directed at Mark for his failure to catch one of his employees' mistakes. Other times, Mr. Russ rages over a piece of negative press regarding a company product.

Today's rant concerns a news article that casts doubt on the efficacy of the company's newest antidepressant. "HOW COULD THEY PRINT THIS BUNK?" Russ screams. "THE GUY WHO WROTE THIS PILE OF LIES SHOULD BE SHOT. HE'S TRYING TO DESTROY OUR COMPANY!! THE NEXT TIME I SEE HIM AT A PRESS CONFERENCE, I'M GOING TO PERSONALLY KICK HIS A—— . . ."

Mark sits silently, holding his breath. He's learned that it's best not to interrupt Mr. Russ when he's yelling. After five minutes, Mr. Russ completes his tirade and Mark is dismissed. Back at his desk, Mark feels his stomach churning. He pops two Tums in his mouth and tries to refocus on his work.

For Mark, Mr. Russ is a Fatal Attraction. What started out as an exciting opportunity to work for a dynamic leader has turned into a series of exhausting interactions. Originally, Mark was drawn to Mr. Russ—his strong opinions, forceful personality, and fiery temperament were appealing, inspiring. Today, Mr. Russ's habitual explosions leave Mark feeling physically ill and emotionally drained. Just one year into his new job, Mark already feels burnt out. "He's always angry about something," Mark complains. "No matter how hard I try, it's never good enough."

Have you ever found yourself in a situation like Mark's? You may have entered a work relationship that showed great promise at the beginning but grew increasingly more difficult over time. Perhaps it involved a charismatic boss, a chummy coworker, or a favored customer. When you first met, you felt drawn to the person; you were excited at the prospect of working together. Over time, however, what started as a positive connection turned into a bitter pill. Interactions with this person left you emotionally upset and professionally frustrated. No matter what you did, you couldn't steer the relationship back to its vibrant beginning. We call this kind of work relationship a **Fatal Attraction**.

Fatal Attractions are very confusing because they feel so exhilarating at first. You literally feel charged when you interact with the other person. Something about their personality entices you, pulls you in. It may be their intelligence, charm, talent, confidence, power, enthusiasm, beauty, education, youth, or social status. You may be captivated by their glowing admiration and respect for you.

Whatever the initial attraction stems from, you enter the relationship on an emotional high. Unfortunately, that "high" inevitably turns south. What begins as a pleasurable connection between two people disintegrates into a painful interpersonal trap for you. The positive qualities that initially attracted you fade into the background, while unforeseen negative attributes crop up and take the foreground: Your charismatic boss suddenly displays a violent temper; you catch the chummy coworker telling a blatant lie about you; the favored customer grows increasingly more demanding and disparaging.

What's most frustrating about a Fatal Attraction in the workplace is that it goes bad due to forces you cannot control. The relationship becomes "fatal" not because of something you say or do, but because the other person changes the rules. Without warning, you find yourself dealing with a different human being than the one you first found so appealing. And you get hooked into trying to retrieve that initial positive connection.

How do you manage this kind of difficult relationship? How do you break free of its grip? Unhooking from a Fatal Attraction begins first and foremost with recognizing that you are in one.

Identifying Fatal Attractions

We all have our own brand of these toxic ties. It's important to understand that a Fatal Attraction for one person won't necessarily be lethal for someone else. Through our work with thousands of people in hundreds of companies, we've identified five common brands of Fatal Attraction. Read each description carefully. As you go over the profiles, consider whether this kind of relationship ever had you in its grip.

The Exploder

This individual is attractive to those who seek approval from authority figures. The Exploder is often charismatic and charming from the outset. He or she exudes decisiveness, determination, and confidence. The Exploder enrolls people to join the team and ride the wave of success.

At first it is an exciting, exhilarating ride . . . until this human land mine hits a snag. A mistake is made, an obstacle arises, and the Exploder detonates. In a flash, a new side emerges that is loud, harsh, accusatory, and irrational. The Exploder can reduce coworkers to tears with a few harsh sentences. He or she will ask rhetorical questions like, "What was I thinking when I hired you?" "How did you ever graduate from college?" "Why am I always saddled with incompetent people?" Explosions may include threats to fire you, sue someone else, or quit.

After the blowup, the Exploder returns to good behavior until the next triggering event. Meanwhile, you turn into an anxious vigilante. Afraid of setting off the detonator, you search for ways to deactivate the next explosion. Instead of performing your job, you're preoccupied with trying to manage someone else's unpredictable behavior.

As in the case of Mark and Mr. Russ, when you work for an Exploder, it's easy to assume that if you could just prevent bad things from happening, the explosions would stop. Every time Mr. Russ erupts over some issue, Mark feels as if he's failed. For people working with Exploders, it is easy to get hooked. While you're drawn to the promise of great success they offer, you become debilitated by their personalized assaults.

The Empty Pit

This bond magnetizes natural caregivers. The Empty Pit requires two players:

1. The Pit—a seemingly kind person who is weighed down with personal problems.
2. You—a person who feels drawn to help people who are experiencing hardship.

Early in the relationship, the Pit exposes you to one or more of his or her difficulties. It may involve a chronic health condition, money woes, mean-spirited family members, a negligent landlord, or a difficult intimate relationship.

The individual solicits your sympathy and basks in your emotional support. In exchange for your kindness, the Empty Pit compliments you on your wisdom and appreciates your compassion. He or she then proceeds to lean on you more and more, revealing other personal plights—sudden injuries, broken pipes, overdue alimony, persecuting neighbors, and so on.

Each request for your ear comes with a plea and a smile. Each confession of a problem ends with you giving away more of your time, energy, and psychic space. Always eager for your counsel, the Empty Pit rarely follows your advice. While you want to be helpful, you begin to feel like an emotional dumping ground.

As the Pit's needs for your attention multiply, the boundaries between your professional and personal worlds begin to blur. You may receive phone calls at your home on weekends or during evening hours. The Pit may ask you for small financial loans or legal advice. Out of your desire to rescue this troubled individual, you may find yourself inviting the Pit to join you for meals, family events, holidays.

Should you say no to a request for help, the Pit becomes infuriated. Suddenly, your sweet, helpless victim exhibits an angry, petulant side that you never knew existed. The Empty Pit may then label you "selfish," "uncaring," "insensitive," or "heartless." You get hooked—afraid of being the bad guy, you feel bound to continue servicing this person. At the same time, you feel drained and resentful from the weight of carrying another person's emotional baggage.

> Look at Claire, a medical technician for a prominent hospital. She spends hours listening to her coworker Dora, who has numerous personal problems. At first, the requests for advice were flattering. "Maybe I can help," Claire thought. "She seems like such a nice person, and I did study psychology in school." But six months later, Claire feels worn out and irritated. She's given Dora free guidance on everything from salvaging her dismal marriage to repairing her broken self-esteem. "Nothing has changed," Claire grumbles. "She keeps confiding in me, presenting one personal crisis after another. She always implores me to give her advice, but never follows my suggestions. If I'm too busy to listen, she withdraws from me and pouts." Claire unwittingly signed up for two jobs—drawing blood and counseling her chronically unhappy peer.

The Saboteur

This dangerous liaison seduces those who crave admiration and respect from others. The Saboteur enters the relationship as your fan, your admirer. You receive large doses of flattery from this person.

You feel as if someone finally recognizes your value. At the outset, this person appears to understand and respect your accomplishments. Early interactions are full of praise and heartfelt attempts to emulate your behavior.

As time progresses, however, you begin to catch the Saboteur in activities that hurt your professional standing. The Saboteur "forgets" to inform you of a crucial meeting that impacts your professional future. A lucrative account "accidentally" gets taken from you. You overhear the Saboteur distorting something you said in confidence about a colleague—making you look petty or unfair. Suddenly you find yourself feeling and looking defensive.

The Saboteur's interpersonal jabs and stabs are subtle, but consistent. When you confront this "friend," the response is always vehement denial of any malicious intent. Still, with each incidence this person's covert conduct chips away at your sense of confidence and security in the workplace. Even though the Saboteur still showers you with compliments, you start to feel unsafe.

Another aspect of this Fatal Attraction involves infiltration into your key professional relationships. After you introduce the Saboteur to your nearest and dearest colleagues, this individual moves in, gradually preempting your position. You may find yourself on the outside looking in as the Saboteur usurps both friendship and respect from your professional associates.

What becomes increasingly clear with each maneuver is that this person covets your power and seeks to undermine you. The Saboteur feels intensely competitive toward you and yearns for your success. You get hooked—caught between your desire to believe this person's stated good intentions, and the danger you sense from their covert behavior.

That's what happened to Ellen, a senior food inspector for the Department of Health. She felt incredibly relieved when Don first arrived to assist with restaurant inspections in her area. Due to cutbacks in state funding, she had been short-staffed for months. Now she faced a backlog of restaurants that needed to be assessed and either certified or shut down.

As Ellen took Don around to the various food establishments, she noticed that her new colleague was both energetic and ambitious. Don studied the requirements for storing, preparing, and serving food with zeal. He constantly complimented Ellen on her professionalism, and tried to imitate her meticulous methods when executing inspections. With his friendly personality and penchant for detail, Don seemed like the perfect solution to Ellen's problems.

Two months later, however, Ellen overheard Don chatting with their mutual supervisor, Ms. Sutherland. "I want to give Ellen the benefit of the doubt," he confided, "but honestly, I've watched her make a lot of mistakes." Ellen couldn't believe her ears. When she confronted Don, her new coworker claimed that Ellen misheard him. "I was defending you to Sutherland. She wanted to know why we're so behind with our caseload. She doesn't appreciate your level of expertise."

Ellen wanted to believe Don. After all, this was the person who constantly expressed admiration and respect for her achievements. Over the next few weeks, however, she noticed Don spending more and more time in Ms. Sutherland's company. Coincidentally, Ms. Sutherland became increasingly critical of Ellen's performance.

The Pedestal Smasher

This rocky relationship is attractive to those who feel insecure about their capabilities yet crave recognition. As the title indicates, your experience is to be placed on a pedestal, only to have that platform smashed. Here's how it works: For a short period of time, the Pedestal Smasher crowns you with more talent, more business savvy, and more potential for success than anyone else in the company. You feel pumped up and excited. Someone finally sees your genius!

Once you are endowed with superhero qualities, you are expected to use those unparalleled gifts to save the day in some way. This may mean resuscitating the sleepy sales figures of a company product, reorganizing a chronically chaotic department, revamping a faded corporate image, or rehabilitating a slovenly work team. For a while, you can do no wrong. As time passes, however, the Pedestal Smasher inevitably searches for and finds things about you that are not "perfect."

Suddenly you've fallen from the pedestal, and you can't get back up. Now, instead of being a star, you are a sorry disappointment. The Pedestal Smasher manages to find innumerable errors and mistakes in your work, your attitude, your appearance, and your thinking. You get hooked—confused and upset by the fall from grace, you desperately try to replicate the behavior that put you on a pedestal in the first place.

Take Greg, a recently hired package designer for a major toy company. He is surprised to realize that he works for a hyper-critical boss. Greg aced the job interview. Lynnette, his future employer, called his portfolio "Fantastic; the best I've ever seen." Greg left the interview feeling elated. He'd finally found someone who could appreciate his unique design sense.

But six weeks into the job, Lynnette began tearing apart every idea Greg presented. "I thought you understood our products. These concepts make us look mediocre at best. Where's the fresh image I asked for?" When Greg asked for concrete feedback, Lynnette dismissed his request, saying, "I pay you to figure this kind of thing out."

"I don't get it," Greg lamented. "I'm the same guy who had dazzling talent during the interview." For a while, he tried to regain his earlier stature, only to be leveled again: "Where's the pizzazz?" Lynnette complained. "Where's the sizzle? These colors are dull; these images are lifeless. Elmo could come up with more interesting packaging ideas!"

Five months into his new job, Greg spends most of his time lying low and playing it safe. "I took this job thinking I'd continue to amaze my boss with cutting-edge design concepts. Now, I focus on avoiding her harsh criticism." Greg is hooked. Demoralized by Lynnette's constant disparagement of his work, he's losing confidence in his own abilities.

The Chip on the Shoulder

This agonizing association is attractive to people with a fairness orientation. The Chip is often bright and capable, but feels cheated by life in some way. You learn early on about the unfair treatment that created a chip on this person's psychic shoulder. It may have been a missed promotion, a lack of formal education, uncaring parents, societal prejudice, economic hardship, or lost opportunities.

Whatever happened remains forever in the forefront of this person's mind. At first, you may bend over backwards to give him or her the chance to succeed. In your desire to render justice, you offer this individual many opportunities to excel. Sensing the Chip's disillusionment with past work experiences, you may also strive to win his or her trust and approval.

Over time, however, you find that no matter how generous you are toward this person, you will always be "the other." You had it easy—whether you actually did have it easy or not—and you are supposed to pay for their previous losses.

The Chip on the Shoulder will be nice to you during the early phases of the relationship, and then will turn on you. This change from friendly to fierce confuses you and throws you off kilter. You get hooked by your conflicting desires—on the one hand, you want to give this talented person the break that he or she deserves; on the other hand, you don't like dealing with his or her defensive attitude and erratic behavior.

> *That's what happened to Peter, owner of a gas station. He currently feels trapped by his resentful employee, Ray. Peter hired Ray because he was likable, a whiz about cars, and eager to work. "I needed the help, and he needed a break."*
>
> *According to Ray, he lost his last position as the head mechanic for a car dealership because a coworker falsely accused him of drinking on the job. After that unfortunate incident, no local repair shop would hire him. Ray's story moved Peter, an empathetic guy. He offered Ray work as a gas attendant and agreed to pay his new employee extra for any repairs performed*

on the customers' cars. "I wanted to give the guy a second chance," Peter explains. "Besides, I needed someone with his kind of experience."

Initially, Ray was extremely grateful to Peter. He repaid his kind employer by giving every customer excellent service. He gladly pumped gas, washed windshields, changed oil filters, and performed numerous skillful repairs on vans, sedans, and sports cars.

After a month of stellar behavior, however, Ray's performance began to deteriorate. First, he became incapable of arriving on time. He'd stroll into the station anywhere between a half hour and two hours late. He had some feeble excuse ready if Peter questioned him. Some days, he didn't show at all, leaving Peter holding the pump.

In addition, tasks that Ray previously carried out without complaint became points of contention. He let Peter know that pumping gas was insulting to someone of his professional standing. And of course, customers who asked Ray to clean their windshield or check their oil were "demeaning." If Peter pressed for better behavior, Ray would tell him to back off.

Now Peter begins every day feeling anxious and ticked off. "I never know what kind of mood I'll get from Ray when he finally arrives at the station." At the same time, he's afraid to fire Ray because he'll lose a great mechanic. "When it comes to fixing cars, the guy's a genius," admits Peter. "But dealing with his unpredictable behavior gives me ulcers."

Now that we've reviewed the five most common brands of Fatal Attraction, take a moment to respond to these questions:

- Have you recently been blasted by an office Exploder?
- Have you accidentally fallen into the clutches of an Empty Pit?
- Are you gasping from the invisible punches of a workplace Saboteur?
- Do you know what's its like to be placed on a pedestal only to tumble as it crumbles?

- Have you mistakenly leaned on someone with a chip on his shoulder?

If you answered yes to any of these questions, you know firsthand the exasperation and confusion inherent in a Fatal Attraction.

The Seven Stages of a Fatal Attraction at Work

Whether your Fatal Attraction fits any of the five most common brands or stands alone, the experience of being in one of these toxic relationships is the same. Alluring at the start, they produce high levels of frustration over time. They're energy-draining. They take up too much real estate in the brain. The other person constantly does and says things that upset your emotional equilibrium. Instead of focusing on how to grow professionally or stretch creatively, you become preoccupied with someone else's behavior.

The following is a description of the seven stages of a Fatal Attraction.

1. **Magnetism.** Also known as the honeymoon period, magnetism is the early, intoxicating stage of a Fatal Attraction when both people are on their best behavior and anything seems possible. Magnetism can last for as long as six months. During this time, you and the other person are drawn to each other. Something about your association feels both familiar and exciting. You spend a lot of time together. You have great hopes for what you can accomplish together and how far the relationship can grow.
2. **Consumption.** At this stage, the relationship turns a corner. The other person begins to exhibit another side of his or her personality. You witness conduct that disturbs you: a hair-trigger temper, destructive criticism, backstabbing comments, intense neediness, and so on. You start to question your perception of who this person really is. The relationship now occupies your thoughts, your dreams, and your conversations outside of work.
3. **Rehearsal and recovery.** In an attempt to control your environment and master the interpersonal exchanges within the

relationship, you spend a lot of time preparing for and recovering from interactions. During stage three, you use your friends, colleagues, and loved ones as sounding boards. Often, you'll repeat a dialogue that transpired between you and your Fatal Attraction, just for a reality check. You may ask, "Am I crazy?" "Did I misread the situation?" "What did I do to provoke this kind of treatment?" Your mind spends hours rehearsing and rehashing both real and imagined conversations.

4. **Conversion obsession.** In stage four, you become obsessed with getting the other person to change. Exhausted by the emotional toll this association is taking on you, you insist that the other person convert into someone capable of understanding and respecting your point of view. You want to render justice and make this person see the light. Your mind now spends hours fixated on what it will take to alter the other person's behavior. Your fantasies may include staging a revolt, bringing in an arbitrator, or sending the other person to psychotherapy.

5. **Post-interactive heartburn.** By stage five, interactions with this person leave you with a kind of emotional indigestion. You come away from conversations, phone calls, meetings, and e-mails feeling jittery, wound up, punched out, overheated, depressed, deflated, or otherwise unhinged. Because the other person's behavior is wearing you down, you start to show signs of emotional battle fatigue.

6. **Allergic reaction.** By stage six, you develop automatic physical reactions to the other person. When you hear their voice or stand in their presence, your body involuntarily responds. Examples include headaches, eye twitches, shallow breathing, churning stomach, tight shoulders, neck pain, back spasms, tingling arms, dry mouth, and hot flashes. Your body expresses its distress in a myriad of ways.

7. **Imprisonment.** At stage seven, you look and feel like a prisoner of war. Part of you is resigned to the negative treatment and can't imagine a better reality. When you talk about your relationship, you sound bitter and resentful. You no longer have hope for a positive outcome with this person. You can't see your

way out and can't find resolution. You feel trapped in a no-win situation.

A VICIOUS CYCLE

While these stages are listed in a certain order, you may experience them in or out of sequence. You will most likely find yourself cycling through some or all of the stages more than once.

Unhooking from Fatal Attractions at work requires **advanced unhooking** techniques. We call them "advanced" because they involve high levels of self-awareness and self-restraint. Can you adapt these skills? We think so, if you're willing to stretch personally in order to grow professionally. Here's how advanced unhooking works:

Step 1—Detect

Before you can treat a Fatal Attraction, you have to diagnose it. The sooner you can identify a toxic tie, the faster you can manage it. We've gone over the five brands of Fatal Attraction and the seven stages to expect when you're embroiled in this kind of relationship. Did you see yourself in any of those descriptions? If so, there's a good chance that you're caught in one of these difficult relationships.

If you aren't sure whether you suffer from the effects of a toxic relationship, your body can be your greatest ally. Even if other parts of you are blind to warning signs regarding tricky associates or treacherous affiliations, your body will register the potential danger. It can act as your Fatal Attraction radar.

Do you know how your body responds to stressful situations? Do you know how it alerts you to people who are hazardous to your health? If you are grappling with a potential Fatal Attraction at work right now, answer the following questions:

When you speak with this person, do you feel . . .

tension in your head?

tightness in your shoulders?

tingling in your arms?

a knot in your stomach?

a pain in your neck?

sleepy or spacey?

Before meetings with this person, do you . . .

sleep fitfully?

feel on edge?

have a queasy stomach?

eat more or less than usual?

tense your muscles?

fight with your loved ones?

After meetings with this person, do you . . .

want to lie down?

want to shut down?

eat more or less than usual?

feel like the wind was knocked out of you?

have a pounding headache?

experience an immense sense of relief?

When you get voice mail or e-mail from this person does your . . .

chest feel tight?

head throb?

stomach drop?

body shudder?

breathing become shallow?

blood boil?

Figure out which parts of your body send you signals. Knowing your body's alarm mechanisms can be especially helpful during the early stages of a Fatal Attraction. If you get the message that a boss, coworker, vendor, or customer could be toxic, you can quickly move to step two.

Step Two—Detach

When dealing with a Fatal Attraction, this second step, detaching, is by far the most difficult to take. To detach means to separate yourself emotionally from the relationship. The goal is to look at the other person from an objective viewpoint. Detaching is a process that requires a concerted, repeated effort on your part. It's difficult because it involves accepting certain facts about your situation:

- **The other person is not going to change.** The Exploder will always explode, the Empty Pit can never be filled, the Saboteur is driven to sabotage others, the Pedestal Smasher will keep putting people up on and breaking pedestals, the Chip will always believe he or she is being treated unfairly.
- **The relationship will never return to its promising beginning.** You can't turn back the hands of time. You won't be able to restore the professional honeymoon you first experienced with this person.
- **You'll probably never receive the acknowledgment or the rewards that you once hoped for from this association.** This last point is especially important, because you're dealing with someone who cannot give you these things. This does not mean you can't learn to function effectively within the relationship. It just means you have to accept that who and what you see is who and what you get. *Note:* Detaching from someone does not require *condoning* poor behavior.

THE DETACH TEST

How do you know if you've really detached? Successful detachment occurs when you no longer expect the other person to change his or her behavior for your benefit. You accept that this individual will continue to do and say things that you don't like; you cannot alter his or her personality.

Try this exercise: Take each of the things that irritate you about your Fatal Attraction and write a sentence that begins with this phrase: "I accept the fact that . . ." (Examples: "I accept the fact that Susan sees nothing wrong with correcting me in front of our clients." Or, "I accept the fact that . . . George is quick to notice my mistakes, but won't admit his own mistakes.") Write as many sentences as you can; each one should describe a personal trait that bothers you. See whether you can honestly accept who this person is.

(If the process of detachment feels impossible to you, we recommend that you enlist the aid of professional help such as a professional coach or a psychotherapist.)

Step 3—Depersonalize

No matter how many twists and turns you experience with your difficult workplace liaison, you need to understand one crucial point: *You are not the first person who has experienced this and you won't be the last.* IT'S NOT ABOUT YOU. When, for example, a Pedestal Smasher begins finding fault with everything you do, it's not because you are hopelessly flawed. It's because that person is engaging in what he or she does best—smashing the pedestal. Depersonalizing can help take the sting out of the hurtful words or harmful actions that your Fatal Attraction subjects you to.

The more you can see the other person's conduct from an objective viewpoint, the less power it has over you. For example, if you're involved with an individual who you suspect suffers from Chip-on-the-Shoulder syndrome, you ask yourself: Does this person seem to be resentful and angry with other people besides me? Does he or she have a long list of grievances from past relationships? Is there always someone or something oppressing this human being? Learning to take their behavior less personally will help you devise an effective strategy for managing the association.

Another important aspect of depersonalizing involves uncovering the negative beliefs you have about yourself that the Fatal Attraction reinforces. If an Exploder calls you incompetent, do you secretly fear it may be true? When an Empty Pit accuses you of being insensitive, do you suspect he or she could be right? As the Saboteur tarnishes your reputation, do you doubt your professionalism? Do the critical statements of a Pedestal Smasher tap into your worst fears that you may not be good enough? Do the angry accusations of a Chip trigger your concern that you may be unfair? Ask yourself, "What negative beliefs about myself does this relationship activate?" Uncovering and deactivating your worst fears (for example, "Maybe I *am* stupid," or "I must be lazy") will greatly reduce your vulnerability to attack.

Step 4—Deal

The final step in unhooking from a Fatal Attraction at work involves devising and implementing a strategy for managing the relationship. Your plan employs basic unhooking techniques. It is based on your understanding that the other person is not going to change and that you need to protect yourself. The most effective strategies focus on the facts of the situation and utilize standard business tools such as job descriptions, interoffice memos, documentation of conversations, and recording of your accomplishments.

Let's go back to our case studies and apply these techniques to each of their challenging situations:

The Exploder

We start with Mark, who is hooked into Mr. Russ, his volatile boss:

Detect: Mark begins by looking over the five brands of Fatal Attraction. He quickly identifies Mr. Russ as an Exploder. He then reviews the seven stages of a Fatal Attraction and sees that he currently exhibits symptoms of stage four (conversion obsession) and stage five (post-interactive heartburn). Mark tunes in to his physical responses to Mr. Russ: He notices that he feels nausea before going to work, and that his head throbs whenever he hears Mr. Russ's voice. Mark also acknowledges that he eats Tums like candy—especially after meetings with Mr. Russ.

Detach: Mark then begins to focus his energies on understanding and accepting his situation. He realizes that if Mr. Russ is an emotional Exploder, heated outbursts are part of his chemical makeup. He practices accepting the fact that *there is nothing anyone will say or do to prevent Mr. Russ from erupting.* As long as they work together, Mark should expect Mr. Russ to call "emergency meetings," where he then vents his anger.

Depersonalize: Mark attempts to stop taking Mr. Russ's behavior personally. He stops believing that he and his staff *cause* Mr. Russ to blow up. He begins to see that Mr. Russ always explodes. Mark and the other employees just happen to be in his line of fire.

Deal: Based on the above factors, Mark devises a strategy for managing Mr. Russ and taking the charge out of their interactions. He comes up with a plan for unhooking physically, mentally, verbally, and professionally. The next time Mr. Russ calls an emergency meeting about a piece of press that infuriates him, Mark walks into the situation prepared to protect himself from his boss's wrath.

Unhook physically: When Mr. Russ walks over to Mark and requests a meeting with him, Mark establishes a one-minute pause. "Just a moment, sir, I'll be right with you." He then takes the time to center himself physically. He takes a few slow, deep, gentle breaths so that he can relax his body and feel his feet on the ground. He gets ready to hear anger while maintaining a calm physical state.

Unhook mentally: As Mr. Russ begins to yell, Mark detaches from Mr. Russ's anger by watching the outburst as if it is a show. He reminds himself that this display is nothing personal. It's Mr. Russ having an emotional explosion. Mark knows it has a limited viewing time; like a sudden storm, it will pass.

Unhook verbally: Mark addresses Mr. Russ's concerns without reacting to the anger. He calmly responds, "I know you're concerned about the press release and we're taking actions right now to deal with it."

Unhook with a business tool: Afterward, Mark writes up a summary of the points covered at the "emergency" meeting, clearly outlining the actions he's taking to address the situation. He sends this follow-up report to Mr. Russ.

The Empty Pit

We return to Claire, the medical technician who feels drained by her needy coworker Dora.

Detect: Claire quickly recognizes that Dora fits the profile of an Empty Pit. When she examines the seven stages, Claire decides that she is already locked into stage seven—imprisonment. She feels resigned to being Dora's unpaid counselor. Claire can't imagine breaking free from Dora's demands. She notices that the minute she spots Dora in the lab, her shoulders become tight. After talking to Dora, she feels tired and depleted—as if Dora has drained her of all energy. Voice mails from Dora make her stomach drop.

Detach: Claire instructs herself to face the facts about Dora. Because her coworker is an Empty Pit, Claire can never give her enough. There is nothing she will do or say to truly solve Dora's problems. No matter how hard Claire tries, Dora will remain unhappy and needy. Claire admits that although Dora *claims* she wants her life to improve, her behavior indicates otherwise. Rather than following Claire's advice, Dora just presents Claire with more problems. Gradually, Claire accepts that perhaps *Dora doesn't want a solution*.

Depersonalize: Claire tells herself, "I am not the first person to try and rescue Dora, and I won't be the last." Rather than worry about how her unhappy colleague will function without her counsel, Claire assures herself that Dora will enlist the aid of another rescuer if she resigns. When Claire pulls away from her Empty Pit, she expects to be criticized. Claire works hard not to be pulled in by statements like: "I don't recognize you." "What's wrong with you?" "You're acting so cold. I thought you were nice." Slowly, Claire sees that just because Dora calls her "selfish" doesn't mean it's true.

Deal: Claire formulates a plan for managing her relationship with Dora. The next time Dora approaches her wanting to discuss a personal problem, Claire begins to unhook:

Unhook physically: Claire takes a deep breath and imagines an invisible protective shield around her body—one that prevents Dora from draining her energy. She also moves a few feet away from Dora to create more physical space between the two of them.

Unhook mentally: As Dora begins to describe her dilemma, Claire reminds herself that she's dealing with an Empty Pit; nothing she suggests will really change Dora's situation. She commits to *not* offering a solution.

Unhook verbally: First, Claire creates a time boundary with Dora. She says, "I'm sorry but I'm behind in my workload today. I can only talk with you for a few minutes." As Dora tells her story, Claire nods and says, "Uh-huh." After a few minutes, Claire interrupts and says, "It's a tough situation, but I know you can figure it out."

Unhook with a business tool: From that moment on, Claire practices sticking to her job description. Because her list of responsibilities as a medical technician does not include counseling her coworker, she can intercept Dora's future requests for unpaid advice by looking at her watch and saying, "I need to get back to work." If she wavers in her resolve, she can keep a time log for one week and record how much time is eaten up attending to Dora's needs.

The Saboteur

We revisit Ellen, the food inspector who feels wary of Don, her flattering coworker.

Detect: After reading about the five brands of Fatal Attraction, Ellen suspects that Don could be a Saboteur. She identifies her own behavior as vacillating between stage two (consumption) and stage three (rehearsal and recovery). Her mind is consumed with conflicting images of Don: On the one hand she remembers overhearing him tell Ms. Sutherland, "Ellen makes a lot of mistakes on the job." On the other hand, she experiences Don constantly professing his undying respect to her. At the same time, she finds herself rehashing and rehearsing imagined conversations with Ms. Sutherland where she defends herself in an attempt to reestablish her stellar reputation as a senior food inspector.

Ellen notices that she has strong physical reactions whenever she sees Don with Ms. Sutherland. She immediately feels a wave of anxiety rush through her body. If Ms. Sutherland criticizes her work, Ellen's face gets flushed, and she feels a pit in her stomach. When Don begins to compliment Ellen, she feels mentally confused and emotionally relieved at the same time.

Finally, Ellen hears a coworker refer to Don as "The Mole." She decides to operate from the premise that he *is* a Saboteur.

BREAK THE CODE

Decoding the antics of a Saboteur is not easy. When in doubt, start investigating this person's behavior and find out how he or she is perceived by others. Past colleagues may give you subtle hints like "watch out," "don't get too close," "stay away," "watch your back." If you hear a coworker whose opinion you value describe someone as manipulative, disingenuous, or not to be trusted, consider that they may see something you don't.

Detach: Ellen begins to accept that, if Don is a Saboteur, he must covet her power and seek to undermine her. She can no longer believe either his compliments or his pledges of loyalty. She needs to view these statements as tactics employed to distract her from the smear campaign he's launched against her with their mutual supervisor, Ms. Sutherland. Hard as it is to fully comprehend, Ellen acknowledges that Don probably feels intensely competitive toward her and yearns for her success.

Depersonalize: Ellen tries to take the sting out of Don's covert attack by recognizing that Saboteurs don't know how to operate without taking something away from somebody else. They don't believe that they can really achieve success on merit alone. As a Saboteur, Don is insatiably hungry for power, influence, and recognition. Ellen understands that she is probably one in a long line of Don's human targets.

Deal: Having come to terms with how her coworker operates, Ellen then gets ready to interrupt his game. Saboteurs must be dealt with head-on. Even though they will rarely admit to doing anything wrong, you must confront them. It is by uncovering their deceit that you stop them from sabotaging you.

Unhook physically: To regain her equilibrium and release the Saboteur's toxins, Ellen engages in exercise—a brisk walk every morning to expel the pent-up anger and disappointment she feels from this relationship.

Unhook mentally: Ellen tells herself that the danger she feels is real. She is not imagining it. When Don compliments her or tries to win her allegiance, she reminds herself not to be swayed.

Unhook verbally: Ellen approaches Ms. Sutherland and, behind closed doors, states the following: "I'm concerned that you may not be getting the full picture of what's happening in our department. I'd like to be notified of any future meetings you schedule with Don so that we can work together to improve our performance."

Unhook with a business tool: Ellen also schedules a private meeting with Don where she informs him that she will be attending all future meetings with Ms. Sutherland until it's clear that he is not misrepresenting her. Next, she employs the business tool of documentation—she keeps a running log of where she goes and what she does in the course of each workday. This log includes all responsibilities performed and all results generated so that nothing will be disputed. Ellen then leaves a weekly report on Ms. Sutherland's desk, which summarizes her activities and accomplishments.

The Pedestal Smasher

We go back to Greg, the package designer for a major toy company. He's hiding from the harsh criticism of his hypercritical boss, Lynnette.

Detect: Greg spots Lynnette as a highly skilled Pedestal Smasher. At this point, he believes he's caught in stage six of the Fatal Attraction cycle. He has an allergic reaction to his boss and his job. Greg sleeps fitfully. He's losing weight. He feels constant tension in his shoulders and back. When he hears Lynnette's voice, his arms start tingling.

Detach: Greg slowly digests what it means to work for a Pedestal Smasher. He realizes that Lynnette constantly puts people on pedestals because she wants to believe that someone else has the answers for her. He starts to understand that, internally, she feels uncertain and insecure. She can't trust her own judgment. Because Lynnette doesn't have a secure hold on her own convictions, she can't sustain a consistent response to anyone or anything else.

Depersonalize: Greg practices not taking Lynnette's criticisms to heart. He reminds himself that he's just experiencing her insecurity projected onto him. As he watches Lynnette interact with other employees, he notices that *no one* whom Lynnette places on a pedestal remains there forever. She builds and breaks pedestals on a regular basis.

Deal: Greg learns that the most important aspect of managing a Pedestal Smasher is to unhook from her devaluing remarks. If he wants to work for Lynnette, he must find ways to defend his value and not let her critical comments sidetrack him. He can do this by documenting his successes and bringing them to her attention.

Unhook physically: The night before a scheduled meeting with Lynnette, Greg makes sure to get a good night's sleep. In the morning, he engages in light exercise (stretches, sit-ups) and brief meditation (five or ten minutes) so that he feels centered and grounded.

Unhook mentally: As he walks into the conference room where Lynnette will be critiquing his packaging design concepts, Greg reassures himself: "Regardless of Lynnette's comments, I know these designs are good." He can tell himself this because he's already conferred with his colleagues and asked two designers whose opinion he respects for constructive feedback regarding his work.

Unhook verbally: Instead of waiting for Lynnette's negative feedback, Greg begins the meeting with this statement: "I took the liberty of running these ideas by two experts in packaging, and they really liked them." This addresses Lynnette's unspoken fear that her company's packaging is not trendy or aesthetically pleasing.

Unhook with a business tool: Greg continues to bring his design ideas to respected colleagues in packaging and design. He always gets constructive feedback before presenting them to Lynnette. He also backs up his designs with statistics regarding packaging trends. He continues to prove to Lynnette that he is moving with the times.

Finally, once a line of packaging actually goes into production, Greg tracks its success. He brings that data to his meetings with Lynnette as well and lets the numbers speak for themselves.

The Chip on the Shoulder

Let's revisit Peter, the gas station owner who feels trapped by Ray, his hostile employee.

Detect: Peter figures out that Ray's behavior fits the profile of a Chip-on-the-Shoulder Fatal Attraction. Peter thinks he's caught in stage three, rehearsal and recovery—he keeps practicing different ways to confront Ray regarding his chronic lateness. He imagines admonishing Ray the next time he complains about pumping gas or servicing customers. Peter wants to tell Ray, "Shape up or ship out!"

In terms of physical reactions to Ray, Peter notices that mornings bring the most discomfort. As he waits for Ray to show up, he experiences waves of anxiety and a pain in his neck. As time passes and Ray is nowhere to be found, Peter's blood begins to boil.

Detach: Peter tries to come to terms with the fact that Ray may be a great mechanic, but his attitude stinks. He has a chip on his shoulder. Peter realizes that Ray approaches every situation as if he is a persecuted victim rather than a responsible participant. Peter accepts that Ray will probably always feel cheated or misunderstood by someone or something. There is nothing that he can do or say to alter Ray's "stinking thinking."

Depersonalize: When Ray complains that pumping gas and changing oil are "below him," or "demeaning," Peter begins to understand that Ray's negative attitude is not his problem. If Peter docks Ray's pay due to lateness, and Ray calls him a "petty capitalist," Peter does not have to buy into the accusation. Peter acknowledges that his personal fears of being perceived as "mean" or "unjust" keep him locked in Ray's manipulative game. He sees that devaluing comments like, "You don't care about your employees," or "You just need me to make you look good," are Ray's attempt to shame him into accepting unprofessional behavior.

Deal: Dealing with Ray begins with stating the obvious: Ray is not doing his job. If Peter wants to unhook from Ray, he must stick to the facts. He must clearly communicate the behaviors he expects from his employee. He must create and implement consequences for those times when Ray does not perform his job properly.

Unhook physically: Peter begins by taking actions to purge Ray's toxic energy from his system. He exerts himself physically by running three times a week and working out at the gym. In the morning, he practices a breathing technique where he breathes in for three counts, holds his breath for three counts, and exhales for six counts. He repeats this until he feels relaxed.

Unhook mentally: When Ray arrives late, Peter tells himself that it is okay to hold his employee accountable. If Ray gets angry and quits because Peter confronts him, Peter and his gas station will survive. He gets ready to be the target of Ray's animosity.

Unhook verbally: Peter begins by setting a verbal boundary. He tells Ray, "It's 10:30 a.m. Your start time is 9 a.m. The next time you arrive late, I'll accept it as your resignation." If Ray tries to argue the point, Peter says, "End of discussion."

Unhook with a business tool: The two best business tools for a Chip are job descriptions and company policies and procedures. The job description must clearly spell out all of the duties required of the job. The policies and procedures delineate the attitudes and behaviors expected of anyone who works for the company. (For more details, see Chapter 7, "Managing Down.")

Peter needs to go over Ray's job description, beginning with his start time, and continuing with all of the tasks associated with being a gas station attendant. He gives Ray a copy of this document and asks if he agrees to do the job. If Ray says "yes," Peter should give him a probation period during which he will be observed and evaluated (we suggest two weeks). At the same time, Peter can take steps to find a replacement so that he does not feel bound to him.

Beware: Expect to Be Tested

Once you change your behavior with a Fatal Attraction, this person will unconsciously redouble his or her efforts to return the relationship to its previous state. The Exploder will apologize, the Empty Pit will flatter you, the Saboteur will try to turn on the charm and lie to you, the Pedestal Smasher will build you up again (preparing for the next smash), and the Chip will try to convince you to bend the rules. Stick to your guns. Do not let these momentary tugs pull you back into the Fatal Attraction's web.

Unhooking from a Fatal Attraction takes skill and practice. Over time, however, it can be done. Use the material in this chapter to identify these challenging relationships in your work environment. Once you know you're in one of these toxic tangos, you can apply advanced unhooking techniques to set yourself free.

FATAL ATTRACTIONS AT A GLANCE

The Exploder

Attracts: People who like dynamic personalities.

Detect: This individual exhibits sudden explosive outbursts that leave you stunned.

Detach: Accept that this person has unresolved rage.

Depersonalize: Know that the explosions will happen no matter what you do.

Deal: Learn to watch the Exploder blow up without being affected. Document all requests generated by the explosion and address with concrete actions.

The Empty Pit

Attracts: People who like to help others.

Detect: Early in this relationship, this individual divulges an array of personal problems.

Detach: Accept that this person really wants attention, not help.

Depersonalize: Know that this person's problems will not go away no matter what you do.

Deal: Stop trying to solve the problems. Document and watch your time. Listen without giving advice.

The Saboteur

Attracts: People who crave praise.

Detect: Pay attention to signs that others may be receiving false, damaging information about you.

Detach: Accept that this person hurts others to further his or her own career.

Depersonalize: Know that this person does not believe that he or she can succeed on merit alone. To move ahead, the Saboteur must make others look bad.

Deal: Stop the sabotage. Find ways to uncover any covert communication the Saboteur may be having with others. Keep records of everything.

The Pedestal Smasher

Attracts: People who like being put up on a pedestal.

Detect: Anyone who serves up large doses of compliments at the beginning of the relationship.

Detach: Accept that nothing you do will reinstate your original statuesque position.

Depersonalize: Know that this person's shaky sense of self is at the heart of the devaluing remarks about you.

Deal: Stop trying to get back on the pedestal. Focus on getting approval, encouragement, and support from other sources. Wage a positive campaign for yourself.

The Chip on the Shoulder

Attracts: People with a sense of fairness; who want to make things right.

Detect: Anyone who repeatedly tells stories of being wronged and/or slighted by others.

Detach: Accept that you cannot alter this person's "stinking thinking."

Depersonalize: Understand that any demands made by you will be perceived by the Chip as unfair.

Deal: Stick to the facts. Refer to job descriptions, policies, and procedures. If the Chip cannot play by the rules, document his or her behavior and look for a replacement.

5

Managing Up—Taking Control

Chop your own wood, and it will warm you twice.
—*Henry Ford*

THE FIVE PIVOTAL PRACTICES OF MANAGING UP

1. Train your boss to meet with you regularly.
2. Come to every meeting with a detailed agenda.
3. Keep a pulse on your boss's changing priorities.
4. Anticipate problems and offer solutions.
5. Always be prepared to give a status report on your projects.

THE HIGH FIVE OF MANAGING UP

1. Be on time or early for the start of your day.
2. Be a gatekeeper and keep away unwanted time-eaters.
3. Create systems so that others can find things when you're not around.
4. Keep confidential information where it belongs.
5. Underpromise and overdeliver.

Alec is the Web programmer for a fast-growing Web site design firm. He's currently building a site for a prominent grocery store chain. He needs to meet with his boss, Steve, to go over some glitches in the production process.

At 9 a.m. on Monday morning, Alec knocks on Steve's office door. "Do you have a minute?" he asks. Steve waves him in, but seems noticeably distracted. He has a phone in one hand, unopened mail in the other. His eyes are scanning e-mails on his laptop computer. Alec asks if Steve has a few minutes to discuss the grocery chain Web site. "Not now," Steve replies. "Schedule a meeting with my secretary."

Alec follows Steve's instructions and schedules a meeting for 3 p.m. Wednesday afternoon. This time, when he arrives at the appointed time, he learns that Steve is tied up in a new business presentation. Concerned about falling behind in production, Alec schedules yet another meeting with Steve for the following week.

When they finally sit down together, Alec gives Steve a status report that includes the problems he's grappling with concerning the construction of the grocery chain Web site. Halfway through the report, Steve becomes visibly agitated. "Why didn't you tell me this last week?" he interrupts. "I just spoke with the client and they're expecting a completed site any day now!"

Alec starts to defend himself: "I tried to meet with you twice last week—" but Steve shakes his head and waves him out of his office. "Go away. I've got to do some damage control for your project."

Alec just got hooked into a losing position. Even though he approached his boss earlier to discuss the grocery chain project, he now finds himself in the deadline doghouse. Alec has a decision to make: Either he can label Steve a lousy listener and walk away in a blaze of self-righteous anger, or he can unhook from his distressing situation by learning how to Manage Up.

Time and again we encounter bosses like Steve whose management style is less than perfect. In fact, many employees classify the people who oversee their work as "terrible." The enormous frustration that individuals experience when dealing with unskilled managers can trigger sleepless nights, anxiety attacks, depression, headaches, ulcers, fights with coworkers, absenteeism, overworking, and even substance abuse.

We've discovered that there are really two kinds of management in business: Managing Down and Managing Up. Managing Down refers to the traditional form of management—taking charge of your staff. Managing Up involves managing the people in positions of authority above you, especially your boss. *The less adept your boss is at Managing Down, the more important Managing Up becomes.*

How often have you listened to friends gripe about the people who manage them? How many dinner parties have you attended where the conversation inevitably leads to woeful tales about horrible bosses? How many times have you overheard exasperated coworkers repeat and rehash frustrating encounters with their inept supervisors?

While the complaints and coping mechanisms that arise in response to being poorly managed are understandable, they do nothing to improve the overall situation. Managing Up offers concrete solutions to the challenge of working for a less-than-perfect boss. Instead of concentrating on your supervisor's shortcomings, Managing Up focuses on improving and regulating interactions between the two of you. It gives you tools to avoid the common pitfalls between employees and their employers.

Why Are There So Many Poor Managers?

Unfortunately, many of the people responsible for guiding and directing the work of others are ill-equipped for the job. This is because companies promote for a variety of reasons—the least of which is the ability to manage. Three common reasons for upgrading an employee to manager status are:

1. Technical expertise—the most accomplished medical researcher may be promoted to head up a research lab. That person knows everything about bacteria but nothing about people.

2. Seniority—the senior salesperson for a jeans manufacturer may be elevated to sales manager based on longevity, not capability.
3. Political reasons—A junior accountant who teams up with the company president for golf tournaments may advance quickly to a supervisory position because of his impressive golf score, not his winning leadership style.

Once placed in a position of authority, it's rare that new managers receive much (if any) management training. Typically, new bosses are thrown into situations where they're expected to sink or swim. Unaware of what their employees need in terms of guidance and direction, these individuals simply assume that people should think and work exactly as they do.

There's a good chance that the person who supervises you never received even the most rudimentary education in basic management techniques, such as how to communicate effectively; how to spell out goals and expectations; and how to monitor and properly evaluate job performance.

In addition to receiving little or no training, many managers juggle dual roles on the job. They manage a department *and* they perform another set of duties. For example, the head nurse of a hospital trauma unit must manage the other nurses on her floor while she tends to her own patient load. The senior editor of a monthly magazine must produce his own stories as he also oversees the work of other writers and editors.

When faced with two sets of responsibilities, the average person selects the more familiar, concrete task. It's more satisfying to check the intravenous tube of a grateful patient than it is to confront two bickering employees. It's easier to craft an interesting article than it is to track down late assignments from lethargic writers.

What It Takes to Manage Up

Given these influences—the fact that many promotions aren't based on managerial aptitude; the fact that, once promoted, most managers never receive proper training; the fact that your boss may be juggling two or more roles on the job—it makes sense that learning how to Manage Up is your best bet for establishing a more satisfying, less frustrating employee/employer relationship.

Before you can learn to Manage Up effectively, however, you must make two important internal decisions

1. You must accept that your boss has limitations as a manager.
2. You must be willing to take responsibility for improving the relationship.

Accepting That Your Boss Has Limitations

Many people get hooked into their own assumptions regarding how the person above them should behave. They operate from a set of beliefs about how a good boss would treat them. See if you can relate to any of these statements:

My boss should . . .

    be more organized

    know how to delegate

    spell out what is expected of me

    give me some time and attention

    appreciate me more

    give me positive feedback

    protect me from unfair criticism

    give me credit for the work I do

    not show favoritism

    be respectful of my time

    care about my well-being

In theory, a skilled manager could fulfill these expectations. In reality, most people in positions of authority fall short in one or several areas. Even seasoned managers find it challenging to live up to such standards. You have a choice. You can either stay within the ranks of the complaining workforce or you can make your life easier by acknowledging your boss's shortcomings and Managing Up.

Taking Responsibility for Improving the Relationship

Many employees are waiting for their managers to change. You may wish that your mean, uncaring, unappreciative boss would transform into a kinder, more caring, and more appreciative human being. You may refuse to repair the relationship because you didn't break it in the first place. Dream on.

We can state with certainty that unless you take responsibility for improving this association, you will continue to get hooked into emotionally upsetting situations. We can also promise that if you adopt certain business practices you will improve this primary work relationship even if your boss doesn't change.

The Five Pivotal Practices of Managing Up

After counseling thousands of employees regarding hundreds of difficult managers, we've uncovered five key practices that can dramatically improve relations between you and the person who oversees your work. Employees who incorporate these habits feel more empowered and less victimized at work, and they are able to experience a greater sense of satisfaction. They don't want to kill their bosses anymore.

Pivotal Practice #1—Train your boss to meet with you regularly.

This first practice should be considered the cardinal rule of Managing Up. If you truly want to upgrade your experience at work, you must meet regularly with the person who supervises you. Hold regular, consistent meetings with your manager *at a time that is convenient to his or her schedule*. These appointments can be short in duration—no more than fifteen minutes. They will save you *hours* of frustration.

If you're like most people, the only time your boss talks to you is on the fly—walking past your desk, rushing to the elevator, calling in for messages, heading out to a meeting. You may have dozens of quick conversations throughout the day. But none of these short, immediate interactions allows you or your boss the time necessary to communicate or plan effectively. Conversations on the run usually go in one ear and out the other. They are rarely remembered or taken seriously. If you want your boss's undivided attention, you have to schedule it.

A brief weekly or daily meeting creates a forum where you can report on existing projects, review departmental goals, be informed of changing priorities, and troubleshoot problem areas. These meetings can become a venue for securing approval on purchases, airing important decisions, mapping out action plans, and introducing fresh approaches to old problems.

We know you may be meeting-averse. You're probably still recovering from the last futile meeting you suffered through. Perhaps you felt trapped as you sat in a stuffy room with other members of your department. You barely managed to keep your eyes open as the talking heads droned on. We're suggesting something very different from that cure for insomnia.

Your meeting will be brief, organized, and on point. You'll leave with a clear action plan for the week or the day ahead. How do we know this? Because *you* will be running it. Your boss will give you the time if you arrive prepared. Bring any information that will help him or her make informed decisions. Most managers value any activity that can save them time and reduce their workload. This practice will do that for both of you.

Initially, your boss may forget the appointment or double-book the time. Be persistent. Find a way to check in regularly no matter what.

Managing Up Scenario #1

In an initial attempt to Manage Up you ask your boss to meet with you. She agrees and schedules a meeting for 3 p.m. that afternoon. You prepare your notes and look forward to the appointment. Ten minutes before start time, however, she calls to cancel—she's off to put out a fire somewhere.

Wrong response: You say, "Okay," and tell yourself that this person will never be available to meet with you on a regular basis. You resent her for always putting other people and situations ahead of you.

Right response: You understand that training your boss to meet with you is a process. You persevere and say, "Let's find another time to meet. What's the best time for you—early in the morning or late afternoon?" You persist until the two of you settle on a day and time that is feasible.

Pivotal Practice # 2—Come to every meeting with a detailed agenda.

Managing Up requires active rather than passive participation in the planning process. Active employees arrive at meetings ready to update their supervisors regarding current projects, potential problems, new ideas, and sudden discoveries. Written agendas afford a concrete vehicle for highlighting important issues.

Follow these guidelines:

- **Arrive at your meeting with a detailed agenda.** Bring two copies—one for you and one for your boss. Itemize each topic that needs to be discussed.
- **Prioritize problems and questions.** List your agenda items in order of priority. You will retain your boss's attention longer if you start with the most pressing issues and finish with the more mundane as his or her attention is waning.
- **Put everything you need to discuss on your agenda.** If you run out of time, you'll both know what issues have yet to be addressed. It will also save you from worrying about whether you forgot to mention some important subject.
- **Bring any documentation needed to help with decision-making.** If you want your boss to approve a purchase, bring the catalog in which it's listed (include prices and order forms). If you want help in dealing with a difficult coworker, bring notes regarding specific behaviors that you find problematic.

- **Take notes on your agenda and file it for future reference.** Detailed agendas provide important documentation. They serve as a record that you can refer to whenever necessary. Past agendas are especially helpful should you be accused of not performing some aspect of your job.

Here's a sample agenda:

Date: February 23, 2005
Start Time: 9 a.m.
Attendees: Alec (Web site programmer), Steve (VP of Web
           development)

Materials needed: list of questions re: grocery Web site (2 copies),
               ACD site report, software catalog, list of vaca-
               tion requests

Agenda
1. Grocery chain Web site—production challenges
   a. How to create multi-flash
   b. Size and shape of banner ads
   c. Trouble with certain links
2. Updates for ACD site
3. New software needed—options and prices
4. Vacation requests from programmers
5. Jesse's going-away party

Next meeting date:

Start time:

Length of time needed:

Attendees:

Topics to be discussed:

Materials needed:

Managing Up Scenario #2

You arrive at the scheduled meeting with your boss and hand him a copy of your detailed agenda. He glances at the paper, smiles, and sets it aside. He then begins to talk about his favorite topic—fly fishing.

Wrong response: You say nothing and follow his lead. Secretly, you think, "This is so typical. I prepare an agenda and he totally ignores it." You focus on his nostril hairs as he babbles.

Right response: You politely bring his attention back to the agenda. You say, "I'd like to check in with you regarding the items on the list I just handed you." You guide him through each topic, emphasizing the importance of his input.

Pivotal Practice #3—Keep a pulse on your boss's changing priorities.

Many managers assume that you know the order of their checklist, even after it changes. During an average workday, unforeseen events occur that redefine what is most important. A delivery doesn't arrive, a large check gets lost in the mail, a project changes direction, equipment breaks down, or someone drops the ball.

Be an agent who welcomes the challenge of responding to unexpected changes by staying on top of shifting priorities. At the beginning of each day, ask your supervisor, "What's your priority today?" If an early-morning check-in won't fly, try communicating via e-mail. Join forces with your boss to create some kind of simple method whereby you can stay abreast of his or her primary concerns.

Checking in at the beginning of every workday will prevent you from wasting time on tasks that aren't relevant to your boss's agenda. You'll also win points for pitching in when the going gets tough. Even if there are no emergencies that warrant your immediate attention, you'll be perceived by the person who supervises you as a team player and a problem-solver.

There are numerous ways to keep a pulse on changing priorities.

Try asking your boss any of these questions:

- What do you need today?
- What can I do for you?
- What else needs to get done?
- What problem do you need me to take care of?
- How can I help you?

We recommend that you stay tuned throughout the day to any sudden pressing issues that may require your or your boss's attention.

Managing Up Scenario #3

You work for an air-conditioning installation and repair company. The opening day of a new shopping mall falls on the hottest day of the year. You arrive at work that morning intending to send out invoices to numerous customers. At 10 a.m., your boss receives a call informing him that the shopping mall's newly installed AC unit just crashed. This is the company's largest account. You see your boss frantically running around trying to address the emergency.

Wrong response: You ignore the situation. You tell yourself, "He got himself into this mess, and he can get himself out." You keep your head down and continue working on the invoices.

Right response: You pick up on the fact that your boss's largest account is in jeopardy. You walk up to him and ask, "What can I do to help?"

Pivotal Practice #4—Anticipate problems and offer solutions.

There's nothing more valuable than an employee who identifies potential sources of trouble and finds viable ways to avert them. Become a tension reliever rather than a stress creator by practicing this skill. Let's say you detect an unfamiliar whirring sound coming from the company copier. Managing Up would involve contacting a competent technician who could investigate the noise *before* the copier breaks down.

NORMALIZING PREDICTABLE PROBLEMS

Every industry has its own set of predictable problems. In manufacturing, for example, equipment breaks down and shipments get delayed. In hospitals, it's not uncommon for medical supplies to run out or for patients to arrive in clusters. Taxi drivers always have to deal with road construction and traffic jams. What are the predictable problems in your industry?

If you can normalize the typical problems, then you have a choice. Either you can continue to be "surprised" when these foreseeable crises arise, or you can address them calmly, understanding that they are unavoidable aspects of your job. You don't have to get hooked by them.

Here are some simple problem prevention actions you can take:

- **Confirm appointments.** Confirming the time and place of appointments can save you and your boss hours in frustration and delays. How many times have you shown up for an appointment only to discover that the location or time of the meeting has changed? A simple phone call or e-mail to confirm important appointments can make a big difference for both of you.
- **Clarify logistics.** Always get directions—even if you think your boss already knows how to get there. Find out how long it takes to travel to the appointment. If a flight is involved, nail down the details—time of flight, name of airline, time of arrival, kinds of ground transportation available. Make sure you secure the name and phone number of the hotel or accommodation where your boss will be staying.
- **Anticipate the reliability of equipment.** How many times have you tried to turn out an important document only to have the printer fail at that moment? Stay ahead of technical difficulties by having routine maintenance performed on all office equipment. We recommend familiarizing yourself with

the people who service your workplace's crucial machinery such as computers, phones, electricity, and air-conditioning and heating systems.

- **Replenish supplies before they run out.** Depending on your job and the industry you're in, "supplies" can involve anything from paper to ink cartridges to computer chips. We recommend that you create an office supply list and update it daily so you're always equipped with the essential materials that you and your supervisor need to do your jobs properly.

Managing Up Scenario #4

You wake up Monday morning realizing that your boss doesn't have her laptop with her. You know she's scheduled for an 8 a.m. breakfast meeting at one end of town, followed by a 10 a.m. sales presentation on the other end of town. You calculate that she won't have time to return to the office, pick up her laptop, and arrive punctually at her 10 a.m. sales presentation. You know that this potential account is important to your boss.

Wrong response: You think, "Oh well. She always forgets things. It's not my problem." You push the snooze button on your alarm and roll over to steal a few more minutes of sleep.

Right response: You get up, suit up, and go directly to the office. You call your boss on her cell phone and let her know that you'll deliver the laptop to her sales appointment.

Pivotal Practice #5—Always be prepared to give status reports on your projects at any time (and we do mean *any* time).

While the person above you may be responsible for managing a department or overseeing a specific project, it's your responsibility to stay current regarding the status of your own work. You never know when your boss will be asked to report on a project that he or she handed off to you. It's your job to be ready with an answer.

Being prepared to report on the status of your work at a

moment's notice is standard fare in the workplace. Why don't most people know this? Because they don't understand how important progress reports are to the people who manage them. In fact, many people experience inquiries about their work as invasive or insulting. Nothing could be further from the truth.

If you're truly Managing Up, then you understand that keeping your supervisor informed regarding the development of any project establishes you as competent, organized, informed, and helpful. It makes both of your lives easier. Always be prepared to tell your boss the following:

- What you are currently working on
- Where you are in terms of accomplishing certain tasks
- How far you've progressed on any long-range projects

Managing Up Scenario #5

Your boss gives you the job of tracking down a package that was shipped overnight via FedEx to the company's Chicago office but hasn't arrived. FedEx's online tracking system is temporarily out of commission, which means that you have to trace the package's whereabouts via telephone. At 11 a.m., she pops her head out of the conference room to ask you where the package is.

Wrong response: You shrug your shoulders and say, "I called FedEx and they haven't called me back." You think, "Calm down. It's just a package."

Right response: You say, "I've been speaking with FedEx and they're in the process of tracking it down. I should have an answer for you shortly."

We return to Alec and his first attempt to meet with Steve. It's Monday morning, and he sees that Steve is distracted and unavailable to really discuss the grocery chain Web site. Instead of waiting to be dismissed, he begins to Manage Up:

- **Change priorities.** Alec states the obvious: "From the volume of phone calls you're receiving, and the stack of mail in your hand, it looks like this isn't the best time for us to meet." Steve agrees: "I really want to review your project, but there's just too much going on right now."
- **Offer solutions.** Alec then offers Steve an alternative: "Maybe we can meet this afternoon at 3 p.m." Steve checks his appointments. "Actually, I'm scheduled to meet with the chief executive of our largest new account this afternoon." Alec persists: "Okay, how about tomorrow. What's a good time for you?" "Early morning, 8 a.m. could work." Alec confirms the time and makes sure Steve blocks it out on his calendar as well.
- **Prepare an agenda.** Alec finishes Managing Up by arriving at Tuesday morning's meeting with two copies of his prepared agenda. Prior to the meeting, he e-mails Steve a list of design questions that need to be addressed.
- **Train the boss to meet.** Over time, Alec establishes a regular meeting time with Steve (Friday morning works best for both of them) during which they can discuss and troubleshoot all of the Web sites currently under construction.
- **Be prepared to give a status report.** At the beginning of each week, Alec hands Steve a list that describes the status of each Web site. As a result, Steve feels more confident and better informed when talking to clients.

The High Five of Managing Up—Advanced Practices

Once you've mastered the five pivotal practices, you can take Managing Up to a higher level by adapting our advanced techniques. We call these the High Five because they create standards of excellence in any workplace. Employees who incorporate these habits become the most valued and respected members of any team.

There's another reason to develop these habits—they'll put your career on a faster track. If you're feeling invisible, if you've been overlooked for promotions, if you feel vulnerable to being downsized, or if you've gotten less-than-positive reviews we suggest you incorporate the High Five.

High Five #1—Be on time or early for the start of your day.

Individuals who show up on time or early for the start of their workday voice one common benefit: Punctuality affords them precious time during which they can prioritize tasks and prepare for the day's activities. As one employee put it, "When I arrive a few minutes early, I can shape my day instead of having the day shape me."

Arriving at your desk or workplace even ten minutes before "start time" will give you breathing room—you can relax for a moment, assess what issues require your attention, and decide where to focus your energy. Being punctual also improves your standing as a reliable member of your work team. It gives your boss and coworkers the impression that you are able to manage your time and are therefore capable of handling greater responsibility.

You may think that only nerds show up on time. But consider what lateness conveys to your employer. Most employers view punctuality as an expression of professionalism, respect, reliability, and eagerness. Chronic lateness communicates the opposite—lack of professionalism, disrespect (for others), low motivation, and unreliability.

What are the things that typically make employees late?

- Oversleeping
- Rush-hour congestion
- Train delays
- A line at your favorite coffee shop
- Getting an unexpected phone call in the morning
- Ironing an outfit you really want to wear
- Thinking you have time to drop off something or pick up something
- A sick child

If you want to improve your relationship to time, begin by building in time cushions. Time cushions are those extra minutes that punctual people naturally allocate for predictable delays such as traffic jams, train delays, lost items, broken equipment, and minor personal emergencies. Time cushions give you a buffer so that you aren't literally running from one event to the next.

Here's what a time cushion looks like:

If you're typically twenty minutes late to work, try going to bed a half hour earlier. Wake up a half hour earlier. Leave your house a half hour earlier. Don't attempt to squeeze in extra tasks like ironing, phone calls, or personal errands unless you block out the additional time needed to accomplish them.

High Five Scenario #1

Norman works the daytime shift as a senior dispatcher for a limousine service. For five years, he's arrived at his job ten to fifteen minutes after his official start time, 9 a.m. Normally, he walks into a room where drivers sit waiting for him, the phone rings incessantly, and his supervisor scowls as he looks at his watch. Tired of rushing in every morning, Norman decides to conduct an experiment: He's going to arrive early for a change.

Low road: Norman sets his alarm for a half hour earlier. When it goes off, he hits the snooze button. "I'm too tired to get up this morning. I'll do it tomorrow."

High road: Norman sets his alarm for a half hour earlier. When it goes off, he drags himself out of bed. "Just give it a chance," he tells himself. Norman conducts his morning routine and leaves the house by 8 a.m. (twenty-five minutes earlier than usual). When he gets to work, he's amazed at how pleasant it is. His early arrival affords him the time to drink his coffee, check his messages, and organize his desk before the fast pace of his regular dispatching day kicks in. Best of all, Norman savors the surprised look on his supervisor's face when he says, "Good morning" at 8:45 a.m.

High Five #2—Be a gatekeeper and keep time-eaters away from your boss.

Protecting your employer's time is one of the most valuable services you can perform. In any work environment there are certain people who qualify as time-eaters. These individuals literally eat up everyone else's time. Time-eaters tend to be oblivious to the notion that you have responsibilities besides talking with or listening to them.

You probably already know the time-eaters who gobble up your boss's time. They're the people who call too often and need too much attention. They're the customers whose endless requests make your supervisor groan. They're the colleagues who turn one-minute questions into twenty-minute conversations. It's your job to recognize these time-eaters and keep them away.

One way to handle time-eaters is to divert them to other departments where they can receive appropriate attention. For example, a copier salesman can be rerouted to the office manager for first approval. The friend of a friend who's seeking employment can be referred to human resources for an initial interview. That needy client who has a thousand questions can leave a detailed, long-winded message with you, and you (not your boss) can respond.

Acting as a gatekeeper doesn't require rude or brusque behavior. On the contrary, skilled gatekeepers act as office diplomats. You can look at a salesperson's materials, check with your boss to see if there's interest, and either make an appointment or politely send the person away. As a gatekeeper, you provide a buffer—giving access only to people who are worth your employer's time.

High Five Scenario #2

Diane works as a paralegal for Rachel Alimony, a prestigious West Coast divorce lawyer. An overwrought client calls for the third time in one day. Diane can tell from the tone in his voice that he needs to vent. She also knows that her boss feels drained from her previous intense interactions with this person.

Low road: She thinks, "Rachel makes the big bucks. Let her handle this guy's hysteria." And puts the call through.

High road: Diane says, "Rachel is held up, can I help you?" The client then proceeds to vent his frustration. Diane listens and takes careful notes. She promises to relay this information to Rachel.

High Five #3—Create systems so that your boss can find things if you're not around.

Too often we meet employees whose method of organizing files, tracking projects, logging contacts, and categorizing data is designed so that only they can retrieve the information. We're not suggesting that you become a professional organizer, we're suggesting that you create systems that your boss can follow.

Individuals who practice advanced Managing Up understand that it's worth their time to devise systems that allow the people who oversee them easy access to their information. Creating systems that other people can use and understand actually makes your life easier. If you are sick or away from the office, for example, your boss and coworkers will be able to find critical documents without delay.

Keeping important information out of your boss's reach (whether on purpose or by accident) can cause multiple problems. Your manager may spend hours duplicating preexisting work, or he or she may end up rifling through your files or searching through your computer in an attempt to locate something. Worst-case scenario, you become the culprit when your boss has to explain why he or she doesn't have an important piece of information. Whether paper or electronic, your systems should allow your boss to fish for any name, resource, or document and find it.

High Five Scenario #3

David is a sales manager for the northwestern region of a greet-ing card company. He's in Colorado on a business trip when the biggest snowstorm of the season hits. The airports and roads are closed. He can't get back to his office in sunny southern Florida. His boss, Claudia, is the VP of national sales. She has a huge presentation scheduled with Wal-Mart for the next day. Claudia needs David's PowerPoint presentation.

Low road: The night before David leaves for Colorado, he finalizes the sales presentation and saves the only completed version on his laptop. After he gets stranded in Colorado, Claudia calls looking for the backup to his PowerPoint presentation. David has to say, "I'm sorry, there isn't one." He then scrambles to e-mail the only finished copy from Colorado. His boss is not impressed.

High road: The night before David leaves for Colorado, he takes a moment to duplicate his sales presentation and put it in the shared server file. He leaves a note telling Claudia where he filed it. When David gets waylaid, Claudia is relieved to find the presentation and the note.

High Five #4—Keep confidential information where it belongs.

This habit separates the trustworthy from the glib in the workplace. It can be tempting to reveal information about salaries, raises, someone else's personal problems, or changes in company policy. But you have to resist the temptation to share confidential news if you want to build a reputation as someone capable of holding sensitive information. You want to be the employee who can be trusted with a secret, not the one who will leak it.

Maintaining confidentiality means that what you hear and see in your boss's office stays there. You understand that when your supervisor confides something to you regarding another employee's situation—whether it concerns positive news like a promotion or negative news like downsizing—your job is to keep the confidence, not spread the rumor. Be a vault.

It can be challenging to maintain silence, especially when you have probing coworkers who sense that something is in the wind. They may try to pry it out of you. It's not easy to refrain from talking about people, particularly when it involves scandalous material like drug abuse, extramarital affairs, or extortion. But the ability to keep private information private will enhance your image as an individual who can be trusted and cannot be bribed.

High Five Scenario #4

Ebony is the executive vice president of a highly respected embroidery company. The company is going through hard times, and Ebony's boss, Dean, has decided to downsize. At the end of the month, he will have to lay off a third of the staff. Ebony knows the plan. She also knows the individuals who will be out of work. She has to keep that information to herself for the next two weeks.

Low road: Feeling burdened by the sad news, Ebony confides in one member of the staff who she believes is trustworthy. Within hours, the news spreads like wildfire. Targeted employees burst into tears. Some members of the staff go directly to Dean to express their distress. Dean is caught off-guard and unprepared.

High road: Ebony keeps the difficult information to herself, and helps Dean set up an organized effort to ease the layoffs with support systems such as unemployment and severance pay. When Dean announces the decision two weeks later at a group meeting, he's able to soften the blow with plans for rehiring everyone as soon as business improves.

WHEN CONFIDENTIAL INFORMATION SHOULD BE SHARED

We trust that if you are privy to classified information that includes unethical behavior or covert activities that could hurt individuals or the company as a whole, you'll bring that intelligence to someone who can do something about it rather than turning it into idle gossip.

High Five #5—Underpromise and overdeliver.

This habit will build your reputation as a stellar employee in any setting. Why? Because, unfortunately, most people tend to do the opposite—overpromise and underdeliver. In our experience, most individuals barely complete their assignments on schedule because they encounter unexpected delays and obstacles on the way to accomplishing their goals.

In some cases, you may have little control over the deadlines you have to meet. Often, however, the inability to factor in delays and anticipate problems causes you or your boss to create unrealistic time frames for completing a job. This brand of "time optimism" generates bad feelings between you and the people who depend on your performance.

The next time you have to determine how long a certain task will take you to accomplish, we suggest you calculate the number of hours you think it should take, and double it. If a problem arises, you're still safe. If everything runs smoothly, you'll be early. For example, if someone approaches you with a assignment and says, "I really need this by Tuesday," you say, "I know I can have it for you by Wednesday." Then if you finish early, they'll be pleasantly surprised.

High Five Scenario #5

Frank is a graphic designer for the arts division of a well-established publishing company. He is given a high-end art history book to lay out. Frank knows that his boss, Sheila, would like him to complete this job in six weeks. Frank estimates that, if his other projects finish up, he could lay out the art history book within that time frame.

Low road: As he begins working on the art history book, he discovers that it is far more time-consuming than he predicted. He works overtime but still delivers the finished product two weeks late. His boss is not pleased.

High road: Knowing that art history books tend to be labor-intensive, Frank convinces Sheila to add a time cushion of four weeks to the original deadline. He promises to deliver the layout earlier if possible. Frank is able to finish his assignment two weeks ahead of time, and everyone looks golden.

MANAGING UP AT A GLANCE

Symptom: You're angry about the lack of communication between you and your supervisor.

Treatment: Train your boss to meet with you regularly.

Symptom: You're feeling frustrated and neglected because no one ever addresses your concerns.

Treatment: Come to every meeting with a detailed agenda.

Symptom: You resent feeling out of control of your daily schedule. You want more predictability.

Treatment: Keep a pulse on your boss's changing priorities. It may not make your day predictable but at least you'll feel more in control.

Symptom: You view questions about your work as unfair interrogation.

Treatment: Always be prepared to give a status report on your projects.

HIGH FIVE CAREER BUILDERS QUICK REFERENCE

Be on time or early for the start of your day—you'll enhance your reputation as a dependable member of any team.

Be a gatekeeper and keep time-eaters away from your boss—you'll gain points for handling difficult people and difficult situations.

Create systems so that others can find things when you're not around—you'll be seen as someone who's organized and able to empower others.

Keep confidential information where it belongs—you'll be known as trustworthy and discreet.

Underpromise and overdeliver—you'll be considered an outstanding addition to any company.

6

Difficult and Extreme Bosses— How to Keep Your Sanity

Now that you've learned how to Manage Up, let's spend some time focusing on those special cases where your boss is in a league of his or her own. This chapter is dedicated to handling those authority figures whose behavior and personality type present unique challenges for any employee.

- Do you frequently feel manipulated by your boss?
- Do thoughts about the relationship keep you up at night?
- Do you overindulge in alcohol, food, or drugs in search of relief from the relationship?
- Is your self-esteem suffering since you began working for this person?
- Have you begun to doubt yourself and your capabilities?
- Do you sometimes question your sanity?

Difficult Bosses

For the purpose of clarity, we're going to make a distinction between two kinds of emotionally challenging bosses—**difficult** and **extreme**. Difficult bosses are those individuals who operate under a different set of rules from "normal" supervisors. These people aren't malicious by nature. They are emotionally and psychologically limited in some way. Each difficult boss operates from a predominant belief or fear:

- **The Avoider**—Fearful of confrontation, this manager avoids any situation that could trigger a negative reaction in others.
- **The Shoot-the-Messenger**—Afraid of receiving certain kinds of negative information, this leader blasts those who deliver bad news.
- **The Sacred Cow**—A likable figurehead, this person fears being exposed as incompetent.
- **Charming Cheating Liar**—Invested in making deals at any cost, this charmer believes that he or she must bend the rules to get ahead.

Extreme Bosses

Beyond "difficult" lies another brand of thorny superiors. These individuals exhibit extreme behaviors that put the people underneath them in no-win positions. Except for some rare cases, working for this breed of boss is a losing proposition. Because they are constitutionally incapable of feeling empathy for anyone but themselves, they tend to run roughshod over their employees in a variety of ways.

- **The Controlling Egomaniac**—Extremely driven and unusually bright, these individuals believe they must control everything and everyone around them.
- **The Absentee**—Physically absent and emotionally checked out, these missing leaders secretly feel that life owes them a living.
- **The Unpleasable**—Emotionally needy yet impossible to please, these demanding directors presume that your only function is to serve them.
- **The Credit Stealer**—Chronically insecure and professionally greedy, these people assume that other people's ideas are fair game.

First we're going to describe the signs, symptoms, and unhooking techniques for managing difficult bosses. Then we'll address sanity-maintaining tactics for handling the most lethal kind of authority figures, extreme bosses.

Level 1: Difficult Bosses

The Avoider

Avoiders fear any interaction that could generate uncomfortable feelings in themselves or another human being. In particular, Avoiders dread dealing with another person's anger, sadness, hysteria, or disappointment. Negative emotions literally terrify them. For this reason, they evade, dodge, sidestep, and steer clear of any situation that could possibly trigger negative feelings.

An Avoider boss may notice employees behaving in ways that clearly aren't right—he or she may witness one employee yelling at or bullying another employee—but fear of confrontation prevents this manager from stepping in to address the situation. Instead, the Avoider does the office version of putting his or her head in the sand. Although authorized to intervene, this boss takes no action.

If you work for an Avoider, a typical scenario might look like this: You approach your supervisor with a complaint about a person or situation. He or she knows that you are presenting a valid problem. As you describe the dilemma, your boss nods in agreement. When you ask, "Will you address this?" the Avoider responds, "I'll look into it," or "I'll get to that." Then nothing happens. During the conversation, this evasive individual truly believes that he or she will attend to your concerns. Unfortunately, that's as far as it goes.

To manage an Avoider, you must be willing to drive the process. You do the work so that the Avoider doesn't have to. You can't wait for this person to act. If you can craft a clever solution to your joint problem, the Avoider will thank you.

> *Sarah is the event coordinator for a four-star hotel. Her boss,*
> *Ted, is the general manager. Currently, Sarah is caught in a*

power struggle with Alvin, the banquet manager. Whenever a client requests a change to the layout of any event, Alvin refuses to implement it. He barks at Sarah, "It can't be done." Sarah knows that it can be done; he's just unwilling to execute the change.

After several weeks of butting heads with Alvin, Sarah approaches Ted regarding her dilemma. "My job as an event coordinator is to service our clients," Sarah begins, "but I can't carry out their requests if the banquet manager fights me every step of the way." Ted listens intently as she describes her interactions with Alvin. This is not the first time Alvin has generated this kind of complaint.

Ted tells Sarah that her anger is justifiable; Alvin should not be challenging a paying client's requests. "Don't worry," he assures her. "I know how to handle Alvin. I'll take care of it." Three months pass, and nothing changes. Sarah and Alvin continue to quarrel. Ted has checked out.

After four months of waiting for Ted to admonish Alvin, Sarah realizes she's wasting precious time. She begins to unhook.

Unhook physically: After work, Sarah goes for a medical massage where she can release the tension in her neck and shoulders built up from dealing with her evasive boss Ted and cantankerous coworker Alvin.

Unhook mentally: When she gets home, she pulls out a notebook and takes an inventory of her situation.

- What's happening here? *I'm working with someone (Alvin) who doesn't like change. And my boss won't confront him.*
- What are the facts of the situation? *My job is to accommodate customers and implement the changes they request. Alvin fights me on every change I present to him. When I complain to Ted, he promises to follow up then does nothing.*
- What's Alvin's part? *Alvin is being his rebellious self.*
- What's Ted's part? *Ted is not stepping in to defend or help me.*
- What's my part? *I'm waiting for Ted to change. I'm expecting him to confront Alvin when he never confronts anyone.*

- What are my options in terms of response? *I can continue to wait for Ted to intervene, or I can devise my own plan to address this situation.*

Unhook verbally: Sarah goes to Ted and proposes the following: "I've come up with an easy solution to the problem we're having with Alvin. I just need you to show up for one meeting between Alvin and me."

Unhook with a business tool: Before the meeting Sarah creates a new form. This document records any changes requested by a client, and requires Ted's signature for approval. Sarah proposes that they all try working with this form. Ted can make sure that the changes clients request are reasonable. Alvin can rest assured that any alterations Sarah asks him to implement have already received Ted's endorsement. Everyone agrees to work with it.

The Shoot-the-Messenger

This is a person who avoids and reacts poorly to certain kinds of information. Shooters will only gun down the people who deliver information regarding a topic over which they feel helpless or ineffective. Most Shooters feel very confident in certain areas and very insecure in others. Common topics that can lead to gunfire include:

1. Money—especially news about decreased revenues, increased expenses, cash flow shortages, growing debt, or lack of financing
2. Personnel—reports regarding behavior problems, employee shortages, employee turnover, staff complaints
3. Production—alerts about faulty equipment, production and shipping delays
4. Sales—news of decreased sales or changing markets

If you are the messenger who delivers information concerning an issue that your supervisor finds overwhelming, you get blasted.

The first phase of working with a Shoot-the-Messenger boss is postponement. Shooters put off receiving difficult information as long as possible. By the time you finally meet with your boss and present the facts, the problem has escalated. He or she then fires verbal bullets at you, blaming you for withholding important information. You go away feeling wounded, angry, and wrongly accused. You're trying to do your job, but your boss refuses to deal with you in a reasonable way.

Shooters are Avoiders in disguise. They avoid news about money shortages, staff problems, or production delays because they don't know how to process the information. It's like asking someone who's illiterate to read a map. To camouflage feelings of inadequacy, that person may yell at you instead.

Once you identify that your boss suffers from Shoot-the-Messenger syndrome, you can decide how to approach the situation. The most valuable action you can take is to become dogged about scheduling and holding regular meetings with this individual.

The goal is to disarm your defensive boss by providing digestible pieces of information. You become both educator and informant. You teach the Shooter how to interpret and use the information you present in a constructive way. But first, this self-protective supervisor must put down his or her gun long enough to take in your information.

Jeff, a comptroller for an international perfume company, finds himself in the uncomfortable position of delivering some tough financial news to his boss, Carmen, the owner of the company. For weeks, Jeff tries to set up a meeting with Carmen, but somehow the meetings always get canceled. First, there's a production problem that needs her attention. Next, an important buyer comes into town, monopolizing Carmen's time. Then Carmen has to leave early to pick up one of her children at school.

Carmen always finds a justifiable reason to postpone her meetings with Jeff. When he says, "We need to talk about some important things concerning the financial side of your business," Carmen replies, "I know, but I have twenty important things to discuss every day regarding my company."

By the time Jeff finally meets with Carmen, he's feeling frustrated and concerned. He shows her a financial report that reveals a very grim forecast for her company. Sales are down, expenses are up, and they owe vendors more than $250,000.

Carmen responds to this news by yelling at Jeff. "How could this happen? Why didn't you come to me sooner? Where's your plan? How are we going to get us out of this?" Suddenly Jeff is the problem. He takes the heat for her financial crisis.

Unhook physically: Jeff takes a weekend at his father's fishing lodge and goes trout fishing. By spending time in nature, he clears his mind and releases Carmen's anger from his system.

Unhook mentally: As he stares at the glistening water, Jeff takes an inventory of his situation:

- What's happening here? *I just spent several weeks trying to get my boss to look at her financial situation. When she finally met with me, she yelled at me.*
- What are the facts of the situation? *Carmen's business is having financial difficulties. She doesn't understand the fiscal end of her business and seems to be afraid of it. She's pinning her current monetary woes on me.*
- What's her part? *By keeping me at bay, Carmen avoids information that intimidates her. When I finally show her the data, she blames me for the bad news.*
- What's my part? *I let Carmen put me off. I allowed her to cancel meetings. I could have worked harder to deliver my information.*
- What are my options? *I can acknowledge that Carmen is clearly afraid of facing the financial facts of her business. She finds conversations about expenses, sales, cash flow, and profit and loss confusing and overwhelming. I can make it my mission to work with her on this area. If she's willing to learn, I can teach her how to interpret financial reports and offer ideas for solving fiscal problems. I can help her stop avoiding crucial information.*

Unhook verbally: When Jeff returns from the weekend, he goes to Carmen and asks for a minute of her time. Behind closed doors, he states the following: "I want to work with you to improve the financial health of this company, but I can only do that if we can meet regularly and look at the facts. I promise to deliver brief, palatable financial reports to you. We can go over them together. From there, we can discuss constructive ways to make this company more profitable."

Unhook with a business tool: Jeff begins to Manage Up by holding weekly meetings with Carmen. As promised, these encounters are short in duration. At each meeting, he presents her with concise, easy-to-read reports. He goes over each document with her, making sure she understands what the numbers are saying. Once Carmen feels more at ease with her business finances, Jeff can e-mail her daily or weekly reports.

The Sacred Cow

Sacred Cows are those people in positions of authority who've been promoted because of longevity, loyalty, personal connections, or family ties. Usually likable human beings, they don't make waves and are careful to comply with company policy. Because they don't cause trouble, there's never a reason to fire them. They get promoted by default.

Eventually, Sacred Cows reach positions of complete incompetence. They don't know how to perform their own jobs effectively, never mind managing the people below them. To avoid being found out, the Sacred Cow does his or her best to maintain the existing systems, and coast.

If you work for this kind of boss, you probably feel extremely frustrated. Afraid of rocking the boat, Sacred Cows resist any kind of change. Your fresh ideas for improving your department, increasing revenues, or introducing new systems get brushed aside. You receive no direction, no guidance, and very little support. Over time, you grow to resent this person because he or she holds you and the department back.

The key to managing a Sacred Cow lies in giving this person what you may feel he or she least deserves—your admiration and respect. Face it, this person is your chief. He or she achieved that position based on factors you cannot control. If you want to be effective in your job, you have to bow down to the blessed bovine.

If you treat this individual with respect, if you convey a sincere desire to make him or her look good, your Sacred Cow supervisor will work with you. On the other hand, if you treat this person with contempt, if you belittle his or her accomplishments, the Cow will block you. As an entrenched member of the company, the Cow always wins.

Miles recently landed a job as exhibit designer for a very large history museum. His boss, Phil, is the head of special exhibits. Miles arrives at his new job excited, and eager to implement innovative ideas. Previously employed at a smaller museum with meager budgets, Miles views this new position as an opportunity to create technically sophisticated and culturally informative exhibits.

At first, Phil welcomes Miles and orients him to his department in a friendly manner. Phil shows Miles around the museum, telling him who is in charge of what, and introducing him to the other members of the special exhibits department. Phil appears to be very involved and on top of things.

Over time, however, Miles notices that Phil is rarely at his desk. For the next six months, Miles e-mails new ideas, leaves articles on Phil's desk, and crafts numerous exhibit models. Phil rarely responds to anything Miles sends his way. When the two of them finally meet, Phil rejects each of Miles's concepts, saying, "I don't think our director would go for that kind of thing."

Miles becomes increasingly more frustrated. Hired to bring fresh exhibits to the museum, he's become a paper pusher of pre-existing projects. He realizes that his boss doesn't have the skills or the drive to make anything new or inventive happen. Clearly, working with Phil is killing Miles from a creative point of view.

Unhook physically: Determined to figure out a solution to his problem, Miles goes out and plays a game of hoops with his college buddy. He works up a sweat and releases pent-up frustration.

Unhook mentally: After the game, he's able to take a mental inventory of his situation.

- What's happening here? *I'm working for a guy who seems invested in maintaining the status quo.*
- What are the facts? *Even though he's my supervisor, Phil has very limited experience as an exhibit designer. He doesn't want to try anything new. He isn't willing to push anything forward. His low level of functioning limits my ability to be creative.*
- What's his part? *Phil doesn't seem to want to grow. He feels threatened when I try to push my ideas.*
- What's my part? *I keep hoping he'll change or get fired. I judge him as useless and in the way.*
- What are my options? *If I look at the picture clearly, I have to admit that Phil isn't going anywhere. He's been with the department for twenty years, and shows no signs of retiring. I can either stew in resentment over his privileged position or I can accept his presence and work with him in some way. If I decide to work with him, my best tactic is to treat him as a Sacred Cow: Be respectful and ingratiating. The less I threaten his power, the more I can push my projects through.*

Unhook verbally: Miles goes to Phil and says, "I'd like to go to lunch with you someday and learn more about your accomplishments." He also makes it a habit to ask Phil about his interests both inside and outside of the workplace.

Unhook with a business tool: After spending time interviewing Phil, Miles discovers that his boss has always wanted to create a truly groundbreaking exhibit about the history of Native Americans in their region. Miles approaches him with a proposal for such an exhibit, emphasizing his desire to share the credit with Phil for whatever he designs. Miles recognizes that if he's willing to make

Phil look good, Phil will help push this project forward. When the two of them go to departmental meetings, Miles always emphasizes Phil's contribution to the exhibit.

The Charming Cheating Liar

These people are the dealmakers and rule benders of the workplace. They see rules as restrictions on their creativity. They are good at selling their point of view, even if it's not true. Charming Cheating Liars (CCLs) are the ultimate feel-good people. They tend to overindulge in sensory pleasures like eating, drinking, sex, gambling, and high-risk adventures. They want everyone in their presence to feel good too.

With "feeling good" as the ultimate goal, Charming Cheating Liars have a very loose sense of morality. They are experts at showering customers and coworkers with compliments. They have no problem telling you whatever it is that they think you want to hear—whether it's accurate or not. These people act as workplace chameleons, changing color and shape to fit the situation.

If you work for a CCL, you may feel both charmed and annoyed. Why? Because on the one hand, your boss regularly tells you how wonderful you are and surprises you with kind gestures. On the other hand, he or she keeps making promises to customers and colleagues that you can't fulfill. After your charming supervisor guarantees the delivery of a new product within twenty-four hours, you have to inform the customer that the product can't be shipped because it doesn't exist yet.

Working for this kind of person is one mop-up job after another. You field the irate phone calls after a charmed customer discovers that he or she was deceived. You dish up excuses when your boss casually overrides company policy. Day after day, your charismatic supervisor will approach you with "just one more favor." Even if you try to say "no" the Charming Cheating Liar won't hear it.

If you work for a CCL, the most important thing you can do is accept the fact that you're working for a dealmaker. This person's ethics will never match yours. Charming Cheating Liars do not change their stripes. If you want to Manage Up, you must be willing to work within their system—trading favors.

Randall works as the head of sales for a large printing company. A high performer, he sets his own hours and follows his own rules. Most mornings, Randall walks in late and hungover. He parks himself in a chair and orders Karen to fetch him breakfast from the deli downstairs. After inhaling his meal, Randall picks up the phone and begins dialing.

No one generates more sales over the phone than Randall. Karen listens to him joking and flirting, charming and cajoling one customer after another. She also overhears him making unrealistic promises so that he can "seal the deal" with each account.

One day, Randall promises a telecommunications company that their four-color, 50,000-piece mailer can be produced and delivered within three days. His bold pledge sends the entire printing shop into a tailspin. To deliver Randall's order on time, other jobs must be delayed. The responsibility for calling all of the other clients to adjust their expectations falls on Karen's shoulders. Once again, she has to cover up for her CCL boss.

Karen enjoys working with Randall but she's tired of feeling used. Even though her boss is a great salesman, he constantly puts her in the position of mopping up after him. When he asks for each favor he pleads, "Oh please, please, please. Do me this one favor. I'll never do it again." This too is a lie.

Once Karen realizes whom she is working for, she can begin to unhook.

Unhook physically: Karen takes a brisk walk home from the office and begins to consider her options.

Unhook mentally: Karen carefully catalogs her situation by asking and answering these questions:

- What's happening here? *I'm working for someone who over-promises to customers, making agreements that I have to fulfill.*
- What are the facts? *Randall will do anything for an order. He*

works from a different set of ethics than I do. He charms people by telling them what they want to hear. Then he pressures me to act as his accomplice.

- What's his part? *Randall confuses lying with doing normal business. He can't make a deal without stretching the truth in some way.*
- What's my part? *I keep hoping he'll change—stop bending the rules and manipulating others. I carry out his orders grudgingly without asking for anything in return.*
- What are my options? *If I accept that Randall will never change, I can start playing by his rules and make deals with him.*

Unhook verbally: The next time he asks Karen to do an outrageous favor, she can say, "I don't mind covering for you but I need Friday off to be with my children." Or "I'll help push this order through but I need a car to use while mine is in the shop." Randall will figure out how to charm, cheat, and lie to get these things for her.

Unhook with a business tool: Because charming cheating liars are rule-breakers by nature, most business tools have little effect on their behavior. The only tactic this boss responds to is making deals.

Extreme Bosses—The Fatal Attraction of Managing Up

There is a type of boss who is so difficult to manage that we advise you to handle it like a Fatal Attraction. As with a Fatal Attraction, these individuals may treat you very nicely at the outset of the relationship. But their early positive presentation quickly deteriorates into a management nightmare.

We call these bosses "extreme" because they act in extreme manners and elicit extreme responses. They have such difficult personalities that you can't expect to feel successful while working for them. If you answer to an extreme boss you probably ride a daily emotional roller coaster. The problem is you don't know how to disembark from the ride.

Like a Fatal Attraction, extreme bosses can lure you into a toxic trap: You keep trying to create a happy ending to that initially hopeful situation. You want to be the one to turn this person around. You want your boss to . . .

- trust you
- show up
- respect your expertise
- appreciate your efforts

To deal effectively with extreme bosses, you need to revisit the advice in Chapter 4, our Fatal Attraction chapter, and employ advanced unhooking techniques. Here's a recap:

THE SEVEN STAGES OF A FATAL ATTRACTION AT WORK

1. **Magnetism.** You're drawn to the other person. You feel compelled to pursue the relationship.

2. **Consumption.** The relationship consumes more and more of your time and energy. It occupies your mind at work and at home.

3. **Rehearsal and recovery.** You spend a lot of time preparing for and recovering from interactions with the person.

4. **Conversion obsession.** You become obsessed with getting the other person to change.

5. **Post-interactive heartburn.** Interactions with this person leave you with a kind of emotional indigestion.

6. **Allergic reaction.** You develop physical reactions to the other person: headaches, eye twitches, churning stomach, tight shoulders, neck pain, back spasms, and so on.

7. **Imprisonment.** You can't see your way out and can't find resolution. You feel trapped in a no-win situation.

UNHOOKING FROM EXTREME BOSSES REQUIRES THE FOUR D'S

Detect: Identify that you are caught in a Fatal Attraction and it's causing you pain.

Detach: Accept that you aren't going to change the other person.

Depersonalize: Learn to take the other person's behavior less personally.

Deal: Devise a plan for protecting yourself and managing the relationship.

Level 2: Extreme Bosses

The Controlling Egomaniac

Most often found in organizations that are built on the celebrity or accomplishments of one person, the Controlling Egomaniac is unusually bright and extremely driven. These individuals frequently launch and run organizations that communicate a strong vision and mission statement. Friendly and charming to people who can do something for them, Controlling Egomaniacs make it clear that the institution, company, or department they oversee is *their* show. Their huge egos require large doses of admiration, and *total control*.

Controlling Egomaniacs often embody the American dream—a self-made man or woman. They may have overcome challenging family situations or survived grueling early-life conditions. They may have moved up through the ranks by working hard and applying their ingenuity. Their resourcefulness and incredible drive eventually put them in positions of power and leadership.

A defining characteristic of this kind of boss is insatiable hunger for fame, respect, and status. As a result, Controlling Egomaniacs tend to overinflate their abilities and magnify their accomplishments. They'll cater to anyone—the press, fund-raisers, politicians—who can enhance their star quality.

Although the personality of a Controlling Egomaniac is often charismatic and engaging, working for this creature is another story. These are the original micromanagers. They don't know how to delegate and can't handle criticism. You may hand your Controlling Egomaniac a proposal, and he or she will tear it to shreds, grading it as if you're a remedial student.

These bosses maintain power and control within an organization by disabling and sidetracking any initiatives that don't originate from them. They are master manipulators. If you work for a Controlling Egomaniac on any project, expect to be battered with questions, overridden in your decision-making, and chastised for every mistake you make. Proving your incompetence secures the Controller's identity as the indisputable ruler of his or her domain.

One of the telltale signs of a Controlling Egomaniac manager is high staff turnover. Because this person is so controlling and devaluing, people come and go at a rapid rate. If you do anything to threaten this leader's sense of power, you get the boot. Anyone who works for a Controlling Egomaniac must obey the cardinal rule: No one can outshine me.

Dr. Dumont is the highly respected founder of an international health organization. He recently interviewed and hired Robert to be head of information systems for his agency. Over the next two years, Robert is supposed to upgrade all its computer networks and software programs.

At first, Robert feels excited and inspired to be working for Dr. Dumont. He believes in this revered health expert's vision— to eradicate malnutrition throughout the world. The doctor admits that computer technology and information systems are alien territory for him. "I'm counting on you to bring us into the twenty-first century."

Robert is committed to replacing the agency's outmoded technology with software and data systems that empower the doctor to raise more money, reach more people, and positively affect more lives. He starts his new assignment by focusing on the agency's archaic fund-raising software. He believes that replacing this pro-

gram could constitute a relatively simple investment that would immediately generate more revenue for the health organization.

After just a few hours of research, Robert finds a new software program that is capable of processing, tracking, and segmenting donor pledges. This program can also produce campaign progress reports and analyze the results of each appeal.

When Robert hands Dr. Dumont his proposal regarding the new software, the doctor finds every flaw—including the typos in Robert's report. "It's too expensive and too complicated. Go back and find me something with real value." Robert returns to his desk feeling a little perplexed. "This program has all the features that Dr. Dumont originally requested," he recalls. "I wonder what he's looking for."

After conducting extensive research and uncovering several more software options, Robert writes up another report and calls to schedule another meeting with his boss. This time, Dr. Dumont insists that Robert meet with each member of his advisory board. "Get their input regarding your ideas first," the doctor insists. "Then get back to me." Several more weeks pass as Robert schedules and holds appointments with each board member.

Having incorporated their suggestions, Robert prepares one more proposal for Dr. Dumont. This time, he recommends a fund-raising software program that the entire advisory board endorses. "This looks good," the doctor concedes. "Now we just have to raise the money to pay for it."

Robert lets out a frustrated sigh, "Dr. Dumont, in my experience it's worth investing in this kind of software now. It will pay for itself in no time, and will enable your organization to raise significant funds quickly." "Don't tell me how to spend my money," the doctor retorts. With that, Robert backs out of the office. "By the time we install this thing," he mutters, "it'll be obsolete."

After weeks of hedging and procrastination, Dr. Dumont finally agrees to purchase and install the fund-raising program. He orders Robert to call a staff meeting to introduce the new software. Dr. Dumont arrives thirty minutes late for this briefing, and interrupts Robert with disparaging remarks like, "I don't *know how this is going to work," and "Are you sure this is the same software program we agreed upon?"*

Six months later, Robert is still trying to implement the new fund-raising program. His boss continues to create obstacles to letting it happen. At the same time, Dr. Dumont periodically criticizes Robert for his inability to complete this one simple project.

In order to deal with his extreme boss, Robert employs the same advanced unhooking technique that we discussed in Chapter 4.

Detect: Desperate to make sense of his situation, Robert begins his own research project—investigating Dr. Dumont's history as a manager. He arranges a lunch date with the doctor's former information specialist. As Robert describes his current experience, his predecessor offers a sympathetic smile. "Dr. Dumont has to control everything—including you. He needs your expertise but, at the same time, you threaten him. Take my word, you can't win."

Robert slowly digests the fact that he's dealing with a Controlling Egomaniac. When he reviews the stages of a Fatal Attraction, he sees that he's quickly moving into stage five, post-interactive heartburn. Conversations with his charismatic boss leave him feeling nauseous, defeated, and deflated. Because Dr. Dumont questions every move he makes, Robert has begun to doubt his own abilities. He sleeps fitfully, and spends his evenings bingeing on junk food.

Detach: As Robert accepts that his employer may be a chronic control freak he begins to relax. He understands that his attempts to introduce a new fund-raising software program into the doctor's tightly controlled universe will continue to be thwarted. Even though his boss *claims* that he needs new information systems, he cannot tolerate the thought of anyone, including an expert like Robert, taking charge of any aspect of his organization. In one way or another, Dumont will undermine Robert's ability to succeed.

Depersonalize: Robert reminds himself of the facts. "I've successfully created and implemented information systems in the past. This situation isn't about my incompetence." He tries to grasp the idea that Dr. Dumont cannot help himself; he's compelled to control, manipulate, override, and belittle the people who work below him. "He did this before I started working for him, and he'll do it again after I leave."

Deal: For the short term, Robert continues to show up for work and slowly push the software project forward. He no longer acts surprised or insulted when Dr. Dumont criticizes him or shoots down his suggestions. He understands that the leader of this health organization suffers from a psychological affliction. In the meantime, he begins his next job search. To that end, he begins circulating his updated résumé.

The Absentee

There is a brand of boss who is there but not there. This individual is noticeably detached from the day-to-day operations of a business. He or she doesn't handle customer complaints, won't pay attention to the company's finances, and fails to hold employees accountable for their actions. We call this extremely lax leader the Absentee boss.

Absentee bosses don't care about the company or department they oversee because, truth be told, their interests lie elsewhere. Your missing manager may be awaiting retirement, battling a chronic illness, or launching a new business. He or she may be obsessed with a personal hobby, consumed by a political cause, or caught in an addiction.

Whatever the distraction is, this apathetic authority gives time and attention to *it*, not the job. Absentee bosses let everyone else make the decisions that should fall under their jurisdiction. If you work for an Absentee boss, you probably assume responsibilities that extend far beyond your job description. To compensate for a missing manager, for example, a machine operator may end up running the entire production line.

Over time, the Absentee boss's lack of participation and leadership results in a survivalist work environment. With no one officially in charge, each employee stakes out his or her own territory.

The company's self-assigned leaders improvise rules of conduct. And the business suffers from neglect.

> Vanessa manages a family-owned restaurant called Bonnie's TexMex. Monica, the current owner, inherited this esteemed eatery when her mother, Bonnie, retired and moved to Florida. Unfortunately, Monica has no interest in donning Bonnie's apron. After years of servicing her mother's hungry patrons, Monica knows that dishing vittles just isn't her cup of tea. She'd rather be a fashion designer.
>
> When Vanessa worked for Bonnie she really enjoyed her job. She took pride in managing the staff, handling the vendors, and overseeing each evening's stream of satisfied customers. Under Bonnie's leadership, the restaurant exuded a certain homespun quality—every meal was prepared with care, and most of the customers were "regulars" who considered Bonnie's TexMex their home away from home.
>
> Working for Monica is a very different experience. The most noticeable change is that the owner rarely appears at her own establishment. At first, Vanessa doesn't mind taking on a few additional responsibilities. She becomes the bookkeeper, menu planner, and staff scheduler. But when Monica refuses to cover for Vanessa on her two nights off, Vanessa grows increasingly frustrated and alarmed. After a period of just three months, employees and systems in the restaurant are beginning to break down.
>
> Because Monica neglects to pay the bills on time, several long-standing vendors stop delivering their goods. Faced with a lack of supplies, including key ingredients for his signature dishes, the chef becomes irate and argumentative. On nights that Vanessa is off and Monica's a no-show, the kitchen and waitstaff attack each other. Customers start to complain about the shabby look of the restaurant and the negative attitude emanating from certain employees.
>
> Over time, the reputation of Bonnie's TexMex Restaurant spirals downward. Vanessa can't believe that Monica would allow her mother's beloved business to fall into such disrepair.

During a six-month period, Monica graces the premises seven times. Each visit consists of her rushing in (decked out in one of her own fashion inventions), signing a few checks, and dashing out. When Vanessa informs her about the angry vendors and the complaining customers, Monica sighs and rolls her eyes. "Can't someone else deal with these problems?" she implores. "I'm tired of hearing about them."

Vanessa begins the process of advanced unhooking.

Detect: Increasingly frustrated and exhausted by her situation, Vanessa tries to ferret out the facts. She realizes that even though she's not the owner, she's carrying the burden of this restaurant business on her back. The actual owner, Monica, abdicates responsibility and doesn't seem to care about the consequences of her negligence. She'd rather be crafting her first fall collection.

Vanessa determines that she's working for an Absentee boss. As the only person who understands how to manage this restaurant, Vanessa feels obligated to salvage the business. At the same time, she knows that the current owner's refusal to pay bills and address customer complaints will continue to destroy it. In terms of this Fatal Attraction, Vanessa estimates she's in stage seven—imprisonment. Physically, she is constantly exhausted. She has insomnia, neck pain, and a constantly churning stomach.

Detach: Vanessa realizes that her willingness to take over responsibilities that belong to Monica is not helping the situation. Part of detaching involves allowing the other person to deal with the consequences of her own behavior. Instead of overcompensating for her Absentee boss, Vanessa tries a new approach. When vendors call asking for payment, she gives them Monica's cell phone number. When customers complain about the condition of the restaurant, Vanessa writes up their grievances and e-mails them to Monica.

Vanessa stops picking up Monica's slack.

Depersonalize: Vanessa tries to look at Monica's behavior from a more objective perspective. She begins to appreciate the fact that this woman inherited a business she didn't want from a parent who insisted on bequeathing it to her. Bonnie must have known that her daughter's true desire was to become a fashion designer. She could have sold her restaurant to someone who really wanted to grow the business.

Vanessa comprehends that she and the other employees of Bonnie's TexMex are stuck in the middle of a mother/daughter power struggle. "I'm sure this isn't the first time Monica has rebelled against her mother's wishes, and it won't be the last." With that in mind, Vanessa takes Monica's refusal to take charge of the restaurant less personally.

Deal: As Vanessa comes to terms with the fact that she has an Absentee boss, she accepts that Monica's behavior probably won't change. Vanessa can repair a leaky faucet, but she can't repair Monica's inability to show up for work. Vanessa has to admit that it is not *her* restaurant to rescue.

For the time being, Vanessa can keep finding ways to hand back the responsibility of owning a restaurant to Monica. If Bonnie's TexMex goes south, that's Monica's problem. Vanessa's job is to keep her boss informed regarding the status of the business. To that end, she can fax, e-mail, or call Monica whenever a decision regarding finances or personnel needs to be made.

Meanwhile, Vanessa can start looking for her next position in a better restaurant with healthier management.

The Unpleasable

Closely related to the Controlling Egomaniac is another extreme boss who can really make your head spin. Gracious at the beginning, this demanding leader will initially endow you with great talent and endless potential. You are a welcome new member to the team. In very short order, however, you begin to feel as if nothing you do is ever good enough. And there is a reason for that. Your new manager is Unpleasable.

Unpleasable bosses have two defining characteristics:

1. They are emotionally needy. They want your time, your attention, and your undying loyalty.
2. They focus on and find the flaw in everything you do. If you make a dazzling presentation and accidentally mispronounce one word, your Unpleasable boss will zero in on that error.

If you work for this kind of extreme boss, you've probably gone through several predictable phases: First, you may have worked hard to solicit praise and approval. Unpleasable bosses have no problem asking you to work overtime, come in on weekends, or travel long distances. New hires usually try to perform these "extras" in an attempt to impress and show their commitment. What these rookies don't realize is that their Unpleasable boss views overtime and weekend workdays as standard operating procedure.

Next, you start to see that nothing you do is ever quite good enough. You notice that from a list of twenty tasks, your supervisor always targets the one item you didn't complete and frowns in disappointment. Even if you arrive on time for an appointment, this critical authority will say, "I thought you'd never get here." As your efforts continue to result in negative feedback and devaluing remarks, you start to feel increasingly defensive and resentful.

The third phase of working for this kind of manager involves becoming increasingly frustrated and discouraged. People who work for Unpleasable bosses tend to turn sour over time. They resent the way their Unpleasable bosses constantly correct, reject, criticize, and find fault with their efforts. "I work my butt off for this person," you cry. "Why is it never enough?"

Payton works as a customer service rep for a refrigerator trucking company. Their vehicles transport milk, cheese, eggs, and other products for dairy farmers in the Northwest. Payton's boss, Elaine, sends him on the road to salvage a damaged relationship with an unhappy customer. Because one of the shipments to a major grocery chain arrived late, this farmer is threatening to use another carrier. This particular dairy business is the trucking company's third largest account.

At first, it looks like the account may be lost altogether. The customer is understandably incensed. It's really touch and go. But after a lengthy conversation and a slight reduction in price, Payton finally secures a contract for another six months. He returns to the office elated at the positive outcome.

As Payton hands Elaine the signed contract, he prepares to receive praise for a job well done. Instead, Elaine finds the only flaw: "You only got a six-month agreement?" She frowns. "You should've have gotten them to commit to a year." With that, she turns on her heel and walks away. Payton stands in the hallway and blinks in disbelief. "I just saved a half-million-dollar account and she complains about the length of the contract." He feels his face redden and his body temperature heat up. "What is her problem?!"

Payton begins the process of advanced unhooking.

Detect: Payton begins to appraise his situation. Working with Elaine is not working for him. In fact, she seems determined to break down his confidence instead of building it up. After each meeting with her, he walks away feeling defeated and deflated.

In terms of the stages of a workplace Fatal Attraction, Payton estimates that he's in stage three, Rehearsal and Recovery. He finds himself constantly rehashing and repeating conversations with her. Even when she's not in the room, he's defending himself. Physically, his back aches and his neck becomes stiff whenever he interacts with Elaine. Whatever he does, it's not good enough. Clearly, Elaine is Unpleasable.

Detach: Payton takes an inventory of the past six months. He sees that his boss has asked him to do countless "favors," only to complain about the results every time. If he looks at the facts of his situation, he has to concede that no matter what he does, she'll never be happy. Elaine's tendency to always focus on the flaws of any situation won't dissipate over time. While he may do excellent work, she may never be able to acknowledge his performance.

Depersonalize: Payton notices that Elaine is Unpleasable no matter who reports to her. It's not about him. She found fault with the work of many other employees before he entered the scene. The next time Elaine devalues one of his accomplishments, he doesn't take it personally. He learns to go to other sources for recognition and appreciation.

Deal: Payton decides to keep working for Elaine while exploring other opportunities in the trucking industry. The next time she asks him to go above and beyond the call of duty, he carefully considers whether he's willing to put in the extra effort. If he thinks the task will enhance his credentials as a customer service expert in the transport industry, he'll do it. Otherwise, he tells Elaine he can't help her and prepares for her predictable disappointment.

THE BEST OF THE WORST

While they may not be capable of praise or appreciation, Unpleasant authorities do give you opportunities to do interesting projects and grow professionally. Some people can work for this kind of leader for a long time. The key to handling these needy yet critical superiors involves setting limits. You have to determine how much time you're willing to give them. You have to define the range of duties you're willing to perform for them. You can spend hours trying to fulfill one request, and your Unpleasant boss will always find the next thing for you to do. You also have to be willing to disappoint this kind of manager when you fall short of his or her lofty standards.

The Credit Stealer

Our final extreme boss is that special employer who delights in taking credit for other people's ideas. This workplace robber will tell you that you are part of his or her team; that your contributions are crucial for the team's success. You'll be encouraged to share and develop your brilliant suggestions. You'll be led to believe that your hard work and ingenuity will be rewarded.

Then, without informing you, the Credit Stealer will share your ideas, proposals, and suggestions with others, assigning him- or herself the role of originator. Should you approach this extreme boss to ask why you did not receive recognition for your ideas, the Credit Stealer will either justify or deny his or her actions. You end up feeling used, manipulated, and infuriated.

"I knew it was a great idea and so did my boss. But I never expected him to take credit for it," cries Marge. A marketing assistant who likes brainstorming innovative marketing concepts, Marge works for a fitness magazine. Originally, she was thrilled to get a job working for Andy, head of marketing and sales. A former fitness trainer to the celebrities, Andy is extremely respected in the industry.

Bright-eyed and eager to please, Marge came up with an idea for a joint venture involving a pharmaceutical company that produces diet supplements. The company could create its own advertorial section for the magazine, generating enormous advertising dollars for the publication. At the same time, the pharmaceutical company could pay to have the magazine distributed to their customers, which would result in an extra half a million readers.

In no time Andy implements Marge's idea. Her clever concept leads to a subscription increase of 100,000. After the enormous success of this campaign, the magazine's executive editor meets with Andy and Marge to thank their department for the brilliant idea. "This may be the single most successful joint marketing venture we've done," says the editor. "I'm so glad you're happy with the results," Andy responds. "It's great when one of my ideas can really crank up subscription sales." Marge sits stunned as her boss takes full credit for her profitable suggestion.

After the meeting, Marge shares her experience with a colleague. "I can't believe he didn't even mention my name," she moans. "He pretended that the entire concept was his."

"Welcome to Andy's world," her colleague replies. "He takes credit for every good idea that comes into this company."

For the next week, Marge is consumed with feelings of anger and betrayal. Until that meeting, everything had been so positive. Andy had encouraged her. He had said things like, "We make a great team," and "I like your enthusiasm." She had no reason to believe that he would steal her idea and take credit for it.

Marge begins the process of advanced unhooking from her boss.

Detect: After a week of waiting for Andy to acknowledge his wrongful ways, Marge realizes her slippery supervisor feels no remorse. She comes to the conclusion that she's working for a true Credit Stealer. She identifies that she's been in stage two, consumption, while trying to process his unethical behavior. She feels physically depleted and confused.

Detach: As Marge gathers more information, she learns of three more incidents matching her own. She realizes that this is standard practice for Andy. With this knowledge, she clearly considers her options. Even if she asks Andy for credit in the future and he says yes, there's no guarantee that he will deliver.

Depersonalize: Marge acknowledges that she's not the first and will not be the last to have Andy steal her thunder. As far as her credit-stealing boss is concerned, she works for him. Any ideas that emerge in the workplace on his time in his environment, he owns. Andy's behavior is not a personal attack on Marge. It's just his way of operating in the world.

Deal: Marge has to weigh her options:

- She can withhold her ideas, which would be stifling but safe.
- She can make sure never to offer an idea unless someone else is in the room. (Even then, there's no assurance that Andy will give her credit.)
- At meetings, Marge can use the larger forum to speak up and take credit for her own ideas—even if Andy is in the room.

- Before proposing a new idea, she can preface it by saying, "I have an interesting idea, but before I tell you, I'd like your assurance that I'll receive credit for it." Andy still may renege on his promise.

The best thing Marge can do is begin circulating her résumé. As with anyone who encounters this kind of corporate culprit, Marge deserves better treatment from a boss who can truly appreciate her.

DIFFICULT AND EXTREME BOSSES AT A GLANCE

Level 1: Difficult Bosses

Operate from a predominant fear or belief.

The Avoider
Fear: Confrontation of any kind.
Remedy: Come up with your own solutions and drive the process.

The Shoot-the-Messenger
Fear: Receiving difficult information.
Remedy: Meet and communicate regularly so there are no surprises.

The Sacred Cow
Fear: Being exposed as incompetent.
Remedy: Share the spotlight. Learn how to work them into your plans.

The Charming Cheating Liar
Fear: If they play by the rules they won't win.
Remedy: Make good deals for yourself.

Level 2: Extreme Bosses

Incapable of feeling empathy for anyone but themselves. You are in a no-win situation. Unhook as if you're with a Fatal Attraction.

The Controlling Egomaniac
What you have to accept: You will never be allowed to shine.

The Absentee
What you have to accept: He or she doesn't care and won't show up for the business.

The Unpleasable
What you have to accept: He or she cannot be pleased and will always find something to be unhappy about.

The Credit Stealer
What you have to accept: He or she feels no remorse about taking credit for other people's work.

TO UNHOOK FROM AN EXTREME BOSS YOU NEED THE FOUR D'S

Detect: Identify that you are caught in a Fatal Attraction, and it's causing you pain.

Detach: Accept that you aren't going to change the other person.

Depersonalize: Learn to take the other person's behavior less personally.

Deal: Devise a plan for protecting yourself and managing the relationship.

7

Managing Down—
Business Parenting

THE FOUR KEY PRINCIPLES OF BUSINESS PARENTING

1. Employees need to know exactly what is expected of them.
2. Employees need consistent feedback.
3. Employees will test their environment.
4. Business tools are a manager's best friends.

TEN SUPERVISORY SHOULDS THAT PREVENT MANAGERS FROM INTERACTING EFFECTIVELY WITH THEIR STAFF

1. I should only have to say it once.
2. They should behave the way I do.
3. They shouldn't make mistakes.
4. I shouldn't have to be their parent.
5. They should know how to prioritize their work.
6. They should know what I need.
7. They should like and appreciate me.
8. They should know that I appreciate them.
9. They should get along with one another.
10. They shouldn't challenge me.

Let's face it, the relationship at work between a boss and an employee often becomes a minefield of emotional misinterpretations. Employees frequently feel unheard, misunderstood, and underappreciated. Managers regularly voice their frustrations with the people they supervise: "Why do I have to monitor them so closely?" "Why don't they just do their jobs?"

After working with hundreds of companies and thousands of staff, we've come to one conclusion: Anyone who oversees the work of another human being ends up in a parenting position. Like it or not, when you're a manager, your employees look to you for many of the same things that children seek from their parents—attention, guidance, correction, and acknowledgment. Success at managing depends on your willingness and ability to develop strong business parenting skills.

- *Jan is the floor supervisor of a large home furnishings store. Recently, she's overheard her best salesperson, Cara, snapping at her coworkers. Jan isn't sure what triggered this behavior. She needs to address the problem without losing her top producer.*

- *William is the dispatcher for a high-end car service. One of his drivers, Larry, is great with the customers, but lousy with record-keeping. His travel logs and expense reports never match William's estimates. Payday always turns into Boxing Day with Larry.*

- *Steven manages the billing department for a bustling dermatology clinic. His people really enjoy working together. Unfortunately, the constant chatting hurts productivity. He wants to cut the noise without slicing morale.*

Each of these scenarios requires some form of business parenting. The person in charge needs to step back, look at the bigger picture, and take steps to correct the situation.

Let's go over each of the four key principles of business parenting and examine what it means.

Business Parenting Principle # 1—Employees need to know exactly what is expected of them.

Employees perform best when they have clearly defined responsibilities, when they know what their productivity goals are, and when they understand what constitutes acceptable versus unacceptable behavior. An important aspect of business parenting involves answering these three questions for each member of your staff:

1. **What is my job?** Normally, the answer to this question comes in the form of a job description. It's your job as a manager to make sure that anyone you supervise reads and comprehends a written account of his or her position.
2. **What is expected of me?** Your expectations of each person who works for you can be communicated by way of performance goals.
3. **What are the behavioral rules and standards of this company?** These should be available to employees via the company policies and procedures manual.

Job descriptions: These written explanations of each employee's responsibilities are critical documents for you and members of your staff. Employees function better and feel more secure when they know how they're being judged and evaluated. As a manager it's your duty to keep job descriptions updated and to make sure that each person working for you knows exactly what his or her job entails.

Goals: These give an employee long- and short-term benchmarks to work toward. Goals need to be specific and measurable. The more measurable goals are, the better you and members of your staff can gauge success.

Vague goal	Specific and measurable goal
Increase number of sales calls.	Increase number of sales calls to twenty per day.

We believe in setting quarterly goals for each member of your staff. It's easier to set short-term goals and monitor success every three months than it is to set long-term goals and wait an entire year to evaluate the results. It's best to put goals in writing, and to refer to them frequently.

You can work with members of your staff to create timelines for their goals. Help them map out the actions needed to achieve each goal, then give each action a completion date. Adjust timelines weekly to incorporate delays and unforeseen obstacles.

Policies and procedures: Whether it's in the form of a manual or a company handbook, each company's P&P is the official document used to impart that organization's rules, regulations, benefits, and privileges. As a manager, it's your responsibility to make sure that you and your employees understand and behave according to company policies and procedures. This is especially important when it comes to topics such as work hours, lunch and coffee breaks, vacation days, sick days, family leave, payday, overtime, benefits, and terms for dismissal.

In large companies, P&P manuals tend to be comprehensive. They often delineate what constitutes acceptable and unacceptable behavior within the company environment. For example, dress code. A possible dress code could read: *"Employees are expected to present an image that is consistent with their role in the company. They must maintain a neat and clean appearance at all times. Jeans, legwarmers, tank tops, T-shirts, shorts, slippers, and any clothing that reveals an employee's lower back or navel area are not appropriate for work, and may not be worn by an employee while on duty."*

In smaller companies, P&P manuals may not exist or may be outdated. As a business parent, it is in your best interest to familiarize yourself with any documentation that exists. If your company's policies and procedures are not up to date, you may want to become a driving force in revising and reinstating them.

Even after your employees have read the company's P&P, you may need to constantly reinforce the rules and regulations by stating them verbally. For example, if the dress code for your office prohibits jeans, and a member of your staff appears wearing his favorite ripped denims, it's your job to remind that person that his attire does not follow the company dress code.

Business Parenting Principle #2—Employees need consistent feedback.

If you want to cultivate consistent conduct from your staff, you must respond to them in a consistent manner. Skilled business parents understand the importance of rewarding good behavior and enforcing consequences for poor behavior. Tools for consistent feedback include:

A. Regular employee reviews
B. Rewards for positive behavior
C. Consequences for negative behavior

Employee reviews: Employees function best when they know what their strengths are and what areas need improvement. If employees are not informed regarding how they can improve, they'll assume that you are perfectly satisfied with their current performance. Employee reviews should be given annually.

Rewards for positive behavior: Part of consistent feedback involves noticing and rewarding the behaviors you want. Business parents refer to this as positive reinforcement. You may want to reward your employees for any of the following:

- Exceeding performance goals
- Showing initiative
- Being helpful and useful beyond one's responsibilities

Rewards for positive behavior vary. Common forms of compensation include:

- Promotions, raises, bonuses
- Education, training, travel

- Comp time off
- Gifts, gift certificates, massages, manicures, facials

Creating and implementing some kind of reward system for the business behaviors you want from your employees will build morale and foster loyalty. Even the simplest forms of appreciation will send a consistent message reinforcing the attitudes, actions, and initiatives you most value in your employees.

Consequences for negative behavior: If you want to be respected as a manager, you must be willing to protect your employees by addressing undesirable conduct directly and firmly. Negative behaviors such as lateness, absenteeism, chronic complaining, low productivity, and constant arguing hurt morale and undermine productivity. Effective business parenting involves finding ways to arrest negative behavior with some kind of disciplinary action.

Possible consequences for negative behavior include:

- Withholding raises, bonuses
- No perks, such as travel, education, expected comp time off
- Tough reviews—stating revised behavioral expectations and negative outcome if not met
- Downgrading of office space
- Demotion (when possible)
- Termination

Sometimes a consequence is as simple as withholding a privilege like company parking or early dismissal on a Friday afternoon. *Note:* We're not advocating a punitive approach to managing. We *are* encouraging you to develop consequences for those who aren't willing to play by the rules.

Business Parenting Principle #3—Employees will test their environment.

Like healthy children, members of your staff will test their environment to investigate the seriousness of any regulation or policy imposed on them. If they are not corrected after breaking or bending a rule, they'll assume that their behavior is acceptable. It's one thing to set policy, it's another thing to enforce it.

Effective business parenting requires a readiness to be challenged and tested by your staff anytime you try to implement a new business practice or set a business boundary. For example, if you decide that you're going to hold weekly staff meetings at 9 a.m. every Tuesday, you can be sure that certain members of your team will find ways to challenge that decision. One person may approach you with a forgotten Tuesday morning dental appointment, while another may call in at 8:45 to see if attendance is really mandatory. When faced with these "tests," it's up to you to persevere:

- Be consistent—Don't water down the message or lower the bar. For example, "Arrive on time" doesn't mean arrive fifteen minutes late.
- Be persistent—Don't let go. Don't let the subject drop, assuming it's resolved. Once you set a rule, you have to watch and see how well employees follow it. They will look to see if you're watching.
- Be repetitive—Say it as often as possible. There is no such thing as "too many times."

Business Parenting Principle #4—Business tools are a manager's best friends.

While families have house rules, companies have business tools. Business tools include many of the business practices we've mentioned already:

- Company policies and procedures, or employee handbooks
- Job descriptions
- Employee reviews
- Goals, expectations, and accountability
- Staff meetings
- Write-ups and warnings

Effective managers use business tools as a means of support. For example, if you believe that one of your employees is not fulfilling the responsibilities of his or her position, refer to that person's job description to prove your point. If you want members of your department to keep one another better informed, stage regular staff meetings where attendees update one another regarding the status of current business initiatives. Used resourcefully, business tools add clarity and clout to any initiative that you want to put into action.

Nine Management Headaches

It's easy to manage good employees. From a business parenting perspective, they are the individuals that you don't have to worry about. Trouble arrives when you have one or more difficult employees under your direction. These are the "disruptive children" of the workplace. They try your patience and disturb other members of your staff. We call these challenging employees **management headaches**.

Read our brief descriptions of nine common Management Headaches. See if you have any of these problematic employees among your staff. After defining them, we'll apply the four principles of business parenting to real-life scenarios.

- **The Chronically Delayed.** Late for work, late for meetings, and late on deadlines, their constant tardiness wreaks havoc on your plans. When reprimanded for their behavior, these individuals improve for a short time. Eventually, however, they usually revert back to the habit of being late.
- **The MIA (Missing in Action).** This brand of employee has a way of missing work due to mysterious health concerns, personal emergencies, and unforeseen events. They frequently take sick days or personal time on a Monday or a Friday. They are the ones who don't show up, and can't make a call because they are stuck on a train, in a tunnel, at a funeral, or on a delayed airplane. Their habit of disappearing without advance warning frays your nerves and leaves your department in the lurch.

- **The Cynic.** Workplace naysayers, these individuals are skeptical of all new ideas. They shoot holes in any positive change you try to introduce. The positive side of these doubting employees is their dependability—even if they disagree with a policy or plan, cynics continue to report for duty. Also, once they get behind an idea, they can faithfully execute it.

- **The Passive-Aggressive.** Afraid to openly disagree with others, these employees say "yes" while their behavior says "no." A passive-aggressive member of your staff will quietly act out in a myriad of ways. If you're dealing with this type of Management Headache, you'll frequently feel undermined even though your employee claims to want the best for you and your department. Common occurrences include "accidentally" forgetting to confirm important appointments, or failing to follow up on crucial initiatives.

- **The Attention Seeker.** Externally friendly but internally insecure, these needy individuals constantly seek your attention and approval. The attention seeker will repeatedly ask unimportant questions just to be noticed. This employee reports his or her accomplishments to anyone who will listen. Attention seekers tend to take up a lot of physical space; like gnats swarming around your head, they always make their presence felt.

- **The Bad Attitude.** Openly unfriendly and hostile, these employees dare you to ask them for anything beyond their literal job description. These unwelcoming individuals are masters of negative body language. Common tactics include: unresponsiveness to greetings or requests, facial expressions of disdain, boredom, or lack of interest, and walking away while being addressed. Bad-attitude employees create dark clouds of negativity in any work environment.

- **The Slug.** Reliable but slow-moving, these employees spend hours completing tasks that others can accomplish in minutes. They do seem to be working; it's just at a snail's pace. Managers tend to avoid giving this type of headache a task for fear that it will take days before they see it again.

- **The Addict.** Whether it's alcohol, drugs, food, or gambling, these employees are consumed by some kind of mood-altering addiction. Addicts exhibit erratic and unpredictable behavior. They often have periods of high productivity followed by periods of foggy thinking, poor judgment, absenteeism, explosive outbursts, and avoidance. The result is inconsistent work and unstable conduct.
- **The Thief.** These individuals possess a value system that says it's okay to take company property. Petty thieves pocket small items like postage and supplies. Full-scale thieves steal larger items like company information, money, and clients.

Let's look at each of these management headaches in more detail. The following case studies describe specific scenarios, and offer solid business parenting solutions.

The Chronically Delayed

Audrey is the manager of a car rental agency. She recently hired Nan to work on her customer service team. Office hours are 9 a.m. to 5:30 p.m. On her third day of work, Nan arrives twenty minutes late. She apologizes to Audrey, explaining that she ran into extra traffic on her way to work. The following week, Nan walks in at 9:15 on Monday and 9:20 on Thursday. She blames these incidents on her faulty alarm clock.

During her third week of employment, Nan is tardy three out of five days. Now Audrey is ticked. She approaches Nan and asks what the problem is. Nan admits her error but confides that she's been looking for a new apartment. At their weekly staff meeting, Audrey reminds everyone of the importance of being on time. Nan nods in compliance.

The next Monday, the entire department has an 8:45 meeting with the VP of marketing. Attendance is mandatory. Nan dashes into the office breathless at 9:15. Audrey is furious. "She knew the company VP was coming this morning. How could she do this to me?" Audrey thinks.

Audrey is hooked. Another person's behavior is driving her crazy. She'd hoped that Nan would correct herself, but time has proven her wrong. Now her employee's chronic lateness feels like a personal assault. For Audrey to unhook, she needs to step back into her role as a manager and practice business parenting. She can begin by applying the four principles of business parenting directly to her situation.

Nan needs to know exactly what is expected of her: Audrey tells Nan what the rules are for starting work. "Work hours are as follows: Arrival time is 8:45 and the workday begins at 9 a.m."

Nan needs consistent feedback: Audrey also reviews her company's policies and procedures manual and quotes the company approach to lateness: "If an employee arrives after 9 a.m. more than three times in one month, that is grounds for termination."

Nan will test her environment: Audrey understands that even though she's communicated company policy, Nan will probably come in late again. Audrey is ready to be tested.

Business tools are a manager's best friends: Audrey continues to lean on business tools for support. She already referred to her company's policies and procedures manual to spell out the consequences of lateness. If Nan arrives after 9 a.m. again, Audrey can write a formal warning. If she's tardy a second time, Audrey can remind Nan about company's policy and say, "The next time you're late, I'll accept that as your resignation."

The MIA—Missing in Action

Tanya, a telephone repair technician for the phone company, is an efficient and competent worker. She can solve almost any problem. Satisfied customers often give her excellent reviews. Tanya's supervisor, Rina, values her employee but she has one major complaint—she can't rely on Tanya to show up.

Tanya's attendance may be fine for a week or two, and then it deteriorates. Two months ago, Tanya came down with leg and back pain. She visited several doctors who couldn't find anything wrong. Within a week, the mysterious symptoms disappeared, but not before they'd caused Tanya to miss an entire week of work.

The following month, Tanya traveled to a wedding out of state. She took Friday off, then accidentally missed her return flight on Sunday. Her airport mishap resulted in two more days of absence Monday and Tuesday. Finally, Tanya lives with her aging grandmother, whose medical emergencies pull her out of the office for days at a time. Six months into the year, and Tanya has already used all of her sick leave, personal days, and vacation time.

Rina likes Tanya, but her MIA behavior hurts morale in the department and wreaks havoc on the scheduling of repairs. The final straw comes when Tanya fails to appear one day. She doesn't call or e-mail. By 5 p.m., Rina is furious. "She has no right treating me like this," Rina steams. At that moment the phone rings. It's Tanya. "Rina, I'm sorry I missed work today, but my grandmother died this morning and I've been making her funeral arrangements."

Rina's fury converts to sympathy. At the same time, she realizes that supervising this unpredictable employee is killing her. One week after the grandmother's funeral, Rina meets with Tanya and begins to practice business parenting.

Tanya needs to know exactly what is expected of her: Rina tells Tanya that she's missing too much work. She hands her a copy of the telephone company's P&P manual. She reminds her about the company rules. "You've used up all of your sick leave and vacation time. From here on in, days out constitute unpaid leave." Rina also reviews company policy regarding nonattendance: "Any employee who plans to be absent from his or her job must call in by 8 a.m. that day to alert his or her supervisor. Failure to notify the company in a timely manner is grounds for termination." Rina cites previous incidents in which Tanya did not comply with this regulation, and gives her three months to improve.

Tanya needs consistent feedback: For the next three months Rina carefully monitors Tanya's conduct. If Tanya misses a day but calls in by 8 a.m., Rina reinforces the good behavior by thanking her for following company protocol.

Tanya will test her environment: One morning, Tanya reverts back to her MIA behavior, calling in at 9:30 a.m. to notify Rina that she can't make it into the office. Rina gives Tanya a verbal warning: "If you fail to call in on time again, I'll have to let you go."

Business tools are a manager's best friends: Rina documents each of the conversations she's had with Tanya and tracks her attendance for future reference. She also consults with the human resources department to make sure she's following company guidelines as they apply to handling chronically absent employees.

The Cynic

For the past thirty years, Judge M. Joseph has run his office chambers like a well-oiled machine. This year, however, a big change is under way. The entire family court system is converting from a paper scheduling system to an online scheduling system. Judge Joseph appreciates the efficiency and speed that this change could provide the slow-moving court. At the same time, he fears that certain members of his staff may not embrace such a dramatic change with open arms.

Martha, Judge Joseph's clerk, has worked for His Honor for twenty-eight years. Her loyalty and dependability as a court services officer are indisputable. Martha's response to most new ideas, however, ranges from "bad idea" to "that won't work." When the court first installed computers in the late 1980s, Martha said, "This is such a waste of money." She became computer-literate, but bitterly complained whenever a glitch in the system occurred.

Now, as the court introduces online scheduling, Martha is the natural candidate to be trained. Judge Joseph sends her to represent his office at the software implementation workshop. Three hours into the training, the judge receives a call from the head trainer. "We're wondering if you could send a more cooperative participant," the instructor queries. "Martha seems extremely resistant to mastering this new system. She keeps telling us why it can't possibly work for your office." Judge Joseph's head starts to throb. "It's hard enough to convert to a new way of scheduling," he thinks. "Why does she have to fight every change?"

Judge Joseph assures the trainer that Martha is capable of learning and implementing this program. He advises the trainer to send Martha back to his office during their lunch break. As he hangs up the phone, Judge Joseph prepares to practice business parenting.

Martha needs to know exactly what is expected of her: Judge Joseph takes Martha out of the office to a local coffee shop. Over lunch, he tells her that she is a valued employee, but he'd like to see her be more positive about change. He emphasizes the importance of supporting this new method of scheduling—regardless of her doubts about it. He cites examples from the past where Martha has resisted new ideas and the harmful effects it's had on the rest of the staff. Finally, Judge Joseph lays out his expectations: "I don't want to hear you and or anyone in our office bad-mouthing this initiative. If I hear you speaking negatively about it again, I'll have to give you a formal warning and document this uncooperative attitude in your annual review."

Martha needs consistent feedback: For the next month, Judge Joseph tracks Martha's behavior. He puts her in charge of showing the other members of his office how to use the online scheduling program. He commends her as each person masters the new system. The judge also begins to invite Martha to meetings that address future operational changes in the court so that she can become more involved with the process of introducing changes to his chambers.

Martha will test her environment: Judge Joseph knows that even though he's instructed Martha to refrain from shooting down new systems and procedures, it's not her nature to be positive. Should he hear her expressing cynicism regarding the online scheduling program, he quickly reminds her that negative remarks aren't helpful to the process.

Business tools are a manager's best friends: Judge Joseph uses Martha's performance review to cite the specific ways in which she can improve her attitude. He sets "ability to adapt to change and integrate new office procedures" as a professional development goal for Martha.

The Passive-Aggressive

Donna owns and runs a family-oriented health club that has 5,000 members. She recently hired Arthur as director of marketing and sales. Donna admires Arthur's intelligence and knowledge in the area of sales, but she often feels undermined by him in subtle ways.

While Arthur excels at meeting with potential members and selling them on the club's services, he lags behind in executing Donna's marketing ideas. When she asks him to update the welcome letter for new members, he says, "Sure." Two weeks later, she asks him for a first draft of the revised letter. Arthur responds, "I've been waiting for you to tell me what you want the new letter to say."

Whenever Donna proposes a marketing activity like launching a promotion campaign or participating in a community event, Arthur nods yes or says, "No problem." Unfortunately, his behavior doesn't match his words. Should Donna ask him about the status of one of these projects, Arthur usually responds, "I haven't done much yet, because I'm not sure what you want." Rather than ask questions or express an opinion regarding the efficacy of the idea, he does nothing.

In the spring, Donna arranges for the club to have a booth at a large community health fair. She assigns Arthur the job of setting up the booth and arranging for members of the staff to work at it. Arthur doesn't seem enthusiastic about this project. At the same time, he doesn't offer any feedback.

Early Saturday morning, Donna gets a call from the club massage therapist. "I'm at the fair, but I can't find Arthur." As it turns out, Arthur has overslept. In addition, the booth has yet to be assembled. By the time he finally arrives, Donna is there too, fuming. "What happened?" she asks. "I don't know," Arthur replies. Donna continues, "I thought we discussed the need to get to this event early and set up the booth." "Well, this was your idea. Maybe next time you should come and set it up," Arthur snaps. As Donna drives away from the fair, she determines to manage Arthur with a much stronger hand.

Arthur needs to know exactly what is expected of him: Several days later, after Donna has cooled off, she meets with Arthur. She goes over the events of Saturday morning and expresses her disappointment with his performance. She states that when they discuss and agree on a plan for any marketing initiative, it's his job to keep to that plan. When Arthur finally admits that he didn't think the health fair was a great venue for club membership, Donna listens to him. "I welcome your input, but you've got to speak up if you disagree with my plans for promoting the club. If you don't like my ideas," she adds, "offer *your* ideas."

Arthur needs consistent feedback: For the next month, Donna meets with Arthur regularly to go over their marketing plan. She checks in on the progress of each project. During these meetings, she lets him know that his opinion is important to her. When Arthur is forthright with his ideas and opinions, Donna thanks him.

Arthur will test his environment: Donna knows that Arthur tends toward passive-aggressive behavior. She watches for moments when his words and his actions don't match. For example, if he agrees to write the copy for an ad that Donna wants to place in several health magazines but repeatedly "forgets" to do it, she confronts him.

Business tools are a manager's best friends: Donna documents Arthur's behavior. She's determined to follow through with termination if he sabotages another marketing initiative. She also interviews potential replacements for Arthur's position so that she'll have backup should she decide to fire him.

The Attention Seeker

Burt works as the head mechanic for a large car dealership. His best mechanic, Karl, embodies the qualities that every boss wants in an employee—he's competent, reliable, tireless, and never absent. There's only one problem. Karl requires a great deal of attention from Burt and other mechanics in the garage.

Karl talks incessantly. He chatters on and on about every detail of his life. From the traffic en route to work, to what he ate for breakfast, to the television shows he watched the night before, Karl reports nonstop. If one of the other mechanics asks an innocent question such as, "What time is it?" Karl responds with a five-minute answer. His relentless narratives distract others and eat up precious time.

Karl also has a way of getting under Burt's feet. At least once a day, Burt turns around and mistakenly bumps into Karl. This eager employee is quick to approach Burt with numerous questions about each car he services. Often, Karl just wants to be reassured that his approach to repairing the vehicle is correct.

Although Karl is an excellent mechanic, his needy personality frays Burt's nerves and drives the other mechanics crazy. Burt decides he has to apply some serious business parenting to this problem employee.

Karl needs to know exactly what is expected of him: Burt takes Karl for a cup of coffee to discuss his future with the garage. Over coffee and donuts, he tells his eager employee that part of his job involves getting along with his coworkers. He explains that Karl's excessive talking in the shop is distracting. "You've got to put a lid on it. When you're working at your station, please refrain from talking. You can converse all you want during breaks and nonwork hours."

Burt also lays out a new policy: Karl must hold his questions to a minimum. "You are an extremely capable mechanic. You know the answer to 95 percent of your own questions. If you have a burning issue, write it down and put it in my box." Burt assures Karl that he'll come by his workstation three times a day to check in: first thing in the morning, at lunch break, and at the end of the day. Burt completes their conversation with a warning: "If you continue to disrupt me and your coworkers you may have to find another job. I'm giving you two weeks to improve."

Karl needs consistent feedback: Karl agrees to amend his behavior. The next day, he goes to his workstation and works steadily without chatting. At the end of the day, Burt checks in and commends him for practicing restraint. "You did a good job today. Keep it up."

Karl will test his environment: On the second day, Karl tries to go directly to Burt with his usual barrage of questions. Burt interrupts him in midsentence and says, "I can't address these questions now. Either write them down and put them in my box or wait until I come to your station before lunch."

Business tools are a manager's best friends: Burt documents his conversation with Karl—including the behavioral changes he's requested. He tracks Karl's conduct for two weeks and figures out whether to hold on to him or let him go.

The Bad Attitude

Margaret, the floor manager of a retail shoe store, needs extra help for their big blowout summer sale. She asks her staff if they have any friends who want to work at the sale and make some extra money. Anyone interested will be trained the week before this three-day extravaganza to learn the basics of shoe sales and customer service.

Ted, the new stock boy, has a friend who needs work and is interested in this short-term sales position. Margaret has Ted's friend, Zoë, come in for an interview. When Margaret meets Zoë, she seems pleasant enough. The fact that Zoë's résumé shows she's had four jobs in less than two years makes Margaret a little nervous. At the same time, the sale is now only two weeks away, and Margaret needs the extra help.

During her week of training, Zoë performs well. She arrives on time, and grasps the job easily, waiting on customers, ringing up sales, handling returns, and restocking just as well as the other floor staff. Her performance seems fine.

On the first morning of the super summer sale, however, something changes. The store is packed with eager customers. Old and new employees are running around one another in the stockroom. Shoes are everywhere, and everyone seems excited— except Zoë. While the other employees are energetic, helpful, and animated, Zoë actually moves slowly, ignoring customer requests regarding various shoe styles. Her facial expression has gone from pleasant to frowning. Her arms are crossed against her chest. She looks at the piles of shoes everywhere with disdain. Zoë's hostile attitude is intimidating customers and infuriating the other salespeople.

In an attempt to salvage the situation and manage her new employee, Margaret takes on the role of business parent.

Zoë needs to know exactly what is expected of her: Margaret takes Zoë aside during a quiet moment and asks her to meet briefly outside of the store. She explains that her attitude is noticeably negative today and it's evident to both customers and coworkers. "This sale requires an upbeat attitude toward our customers. If you can't shift gears within the next twenty minutes, I'm going to have you work exclusively in the stockroom for the rest of the day."

Zoë needs consistent feedback: Zoë apologizes for being moody, and goes back into the store. To Margaret's relief, she is able to put on a pleasant demeanor for the customers. Margaret checks in periodically throughout the day. When a satisfied customer thanks Zoë for being an angel, Margaret gives her newest employee a smile. "You're doing great."

Zoë will test her environment: Margaret knows that even though she got Zoë to improve her attitude during the first day, there's still the possibility that Zoë could become hostile again tomorrow or the following day.

Business tools are a manager's best friends: Although she needs the extra help, Margaret determines that another bout of negativity during the sale will be grounds for immediate termination. At the end of the first day, she calls all of the staff together and lays down this policy: "We have two more days of this sale, and I want all of us to act as a team. Anyone who has a problem with that or who can't handle the pressure of high-volume sales will be asked to leave."

The Slug

Maria is the director of delivery for a home health care supplies company. With the loss of her best employee to maternity leave, she fears that her department is spinning out of control. She still has one employee, Dale, who is a steady and dedicated worker. He asserts that, with a little extra effort, he can coordinate the delivery of health care supplies to anyone who needs them.

Maria wants to believe that Dale can rise to the occasion. As they go over his broadened responsibilities, she reminds him that all orders must be delivered on the day of request. Dale concurs: "Of course."

During the first few days of this new arrangement, Margaret notices that Dale seems a bit overwhelmed. He's constantly on the phone, and there are piles of order slips all over his desk. When Maria asks how it's going, he says, "Fine." It appears that medical supplies are going out the door as usual, so Maria leaves her hardworking employee alone.

Maria arrives on Monday morning of week two to the sound of someone yelling in Dale's office. She walks over to find a normally mild-mannered home health care nurse shouting at Dale for not doing his job. "I have patients who've been waiting for bedpans for five days! That's UNACCEPTABLE!" Dale rubs the back of his neck and tries to calm his angry customer: "I promise you, I'll get to it. We're a little swamped here at the moment."

After witnessing this scene, Maria checks her messages to find five more complaints from nurses, doctors, and patients who have not received their supplies. She springs into action. She

*returns to Dale's office, takes the order slips off his desk, and fig-
ures out which supplies have yet to be delivered. Within four
hours, she makes sure that all requested materials have been
packed and sent out the door.*

  *Maria can't understand why it takes her only four hours to
accomplish tasks that Dale can't complete in one week. Instead
of condemning her slow-moving employee, however, she begins
to practice business parenting.*

Dale needs to know exactly what is expected of him: Maria recon-
siders how she is managing Dale. She decides to spend a day training him. As she takes him through her method of coordinating
health care supply deliveries, she writes down each action so that he
has a clear series of steps to follow. At the end of the day, Dale
knows exactly what Maria expects from him. He also has a written
procedure for reference.

Dale needs consistent feedback: For the next week, Maria checks
in periodically with Dale throughout each workday. She observes
where he is in terms of fulfilling deliveries, and helps him refocus if
he falls behind while handling a complicated order.

Dale will test his environment: Even though Maria has put in the
time to train Dale and check in on him, she knows that he can easily become overwhelmed. She accepts her methodical employee's
need for constant direction and nudges from her. Instead of letting
Dale fall behind again, Maria monitors him carefully.

Business tools are a manager's best friends: Whenever Dale has to
perform a new task, Maria documents the procedure for accomplishing that task. She also meets with him at the beginning of each
workday to lay out his priorities so that the most important work
gets done.

The Addict

*Rick, the production manager for an established costume jewelry
company, relies on Fran, his import coordinator, to communi-*

cate with factories in India and China. It's Fran's job to make sure that the jewelry produced in those countries arrives in the United States intact and on time.

Lately Fran is not on top of her game. She often comes to work late, looking tired and disheveled. Rick notices that she nods off during staff meetings. Several times, he's found her at her desk, fast asleep in the middle of the afternoon. Rick wakes her and tells her to go home, but she insists on staying at work. "I'm sorry. I'm a little out of it because I didn't get much sleep last night."

One day, Rick approaches Fran to find out about a particular shipment of jewelry coming from India. As Fran responds to his questions, she slurs her words. "Fran, you don't sound right. Are you okay?" he asks. "I'm fine," she responds. "I jus' took a cold decongestant thaz got me giddy."

As Rick clears his desk to go home that evening, three of Fran's colleagues enter his office and close the door. "We need to talk to you about Fran," they say. Rick asks them to sit down. Within minutes, he hears information that seems impossible to believe.

Fran's sleepiness, slurred speech, and low productivity are the result of substance abuse. She's addicted to prescription drugs—downers of all kinds. Her three colleagues discovered her "stash" in a box that they thought contained miscellaneous bracelet clasps. When they confronted Fran, she told them to mind their own business. Concerned about her well-being, they felt obliged to alert Rick.

In this kind of situation, a manager must look at the resources available through his or her company. Generally speaking, illegal drugs in the workplace are grounds for immediate termination. However, some companies have employee assistance programs. Others may provide insurance that covers drug treatment. How you handle an employee who suffers from substance abuse depends on your company's policies. Rick and Fran's company offers a medical leave program for substance abuse.

Fran needs to know exactly what is expected of her: The next day, Rick meets with Fran. He tells her that he's seriously concerned about her health and that her performance at work is deteriorating. "You fall asleep at your desk, nod off at meetings, and slur your words when we talk to each other. Your colleagues have expressed serious concern about your mental and physical state." He tells her that she must go to HR and take a medical leave if she needs time to get better.

Fran needs consistent feedback: Rick asks Fran if she understands what he's telling her. She says, "I think I know what you're driving at. I just need a day to think about it." Rick responds, "Give it all the thought you need. The bottom line is you need to get help or we can't keep you on."

Fran will test her environment: The next day, Fran arrives at Rick's office and tries to bargain with him. "Look, I know I've been very out of sorts, but I think I can improve if I just take a couple of personal days to sort things out." Rick sticks to his initial statement: "If you don't go to HR for the help you need, we're going to have to terminate you."

Business tools are a manager's best friends: Rick calls human resources and informs them of Fran's situation. He also documents the many incidents leading up to this point, including the disclosure given by her three coworkers. The following day, Fran goes directly to HR and requests treatment for her problem.

The Thief

> Sal's art gallery is growing fast. Blessed with an excellent eye for spotting trends and purchasing art, he knows what collectors like. Sal enjoys all aspects of running his gallery except for overseeing the finances. Aware of his reluctance to keep careful financial records, Sal's accountant recommends that he hire a full-time bookkeeper.
>
> The day that Sal interviews Gloria, he lets out a sigh of relief. Gloria seems extremely mature and honest. She comes to work

on time, pays all the bills on schedule, and takes full charge of the gallery's finances. Gloria's bookkeeping allows Sal to concentrate on what he does best—buying and selling art.

One Friday, as Sal signs the company paychecks, he does a double take. He spots two paychecks made out to Gloria. As he hands the checks back to Gloria, he shares his observation: "I may be hallucinating, but I think I saw two paychecks made out to you." Gloria's face turns beet red. His calm bookkeeper becomes noticeably flustered. "Oh, Sal, let me take care of that. I must have made a mistake." With that, she rips one of the two checks into tiny pieces, adding, "I'm so sorry. I don't usually make mistakes."

After she leaves for the day, Sal goes into the financial files and finds bank statements from the last six months. To his horror, there are several duplicate checks made out to Gloria. He then goes through the checkbook and discovers that Gloria has helped herself to two paychecks on a regular basis. She's also written gallery checks to pay her personal credit card bills.

Gloria needs to know exactly what is expected of her: In this case, the only action to take is to fire Gloria. At the same time, Sal needs to press charges for the crimes she's committed. Trembling from the shock of it all, Sal picks up the phone and dials the police.

Supervisory Shoulds

If you find yourself resisting the concept of business parenting, we understand. It takes a lot of effort to carry out these principles on a consistent basis. At the same time, you could save yourself hours of frustration and pain by utilizing our simple business parenting principles.

Sometimes the refusal to experiment with business parenting techniques stems from wanting to hold on to certain beliefs about how the people you supervise should behave. For example, if you believe that employees should know how to prioritize their own work, then you will be very reluctant to help them set priorities on a daily or weekly basis. We call the faulty assumptions that keep managers hooked into difficult employer/employee situations **Supervisory Shoulds**.

Here are ten of the most common Supervisory Shoulds:

1. I should only have to say it once.
2. They should behave the way I do.
3. They shouldn't make mistakes.
4. I shouldn't have to be their parent.
5. They should know how to prioritize their work.
6. They should know what I need.
7. They should like and appreciate me.
8. They should know that I appreciate them.
9. They should get along with one another.
10. They shouldn't challenge me.

Supervisory Shoulds create fertile ground for feeling angry, frustrated, betrayed, or manipulated by the people who report to you. Each of these assumptions increases the likelihood of any manager getting caught in unproductive power struggles with members of his or her staff. The key to unhooking from a Supervisory Should is to uncover it. Once uncovered, you can decide whether you're willing to let it go. The following case studies depict real-life situations in which managers unearth their own Shoulds and take concrete steps to create a different, better outcome.

1. I should only have to say it once.

Symptom: You find yourself irritated whenever you have to repeat something you've already said.

Solution: Accept that business parenting is an ongoing process. Repetition is part of the game. Repetition is part of the game. Repetition is part of the game.

Scenario: *It's 9:30 a.m. and Shirley is steaming. Two weeks ago, she established a new system for her employees to sign in each morning, and* only half of them are complying. "At the beginning of this month, I dedicated an entire staff meeting to introducing this new system. Now it's halfway into the month. What does it take for these guys to follow a simple procedure?" In an attempt to calm herself down, Shirley takes a quick Supervisory Should inventory:

- What's happening here? *I instituted a new sign-in system, and only half of my employees are adhering to it.*
- What's their part? *They aren't remembering what we discussed. They don't seem to understand the importance of this new procedure.*
- What's my part? *Having explained this new way of signing in once, I expect everyone to follow it.*
- From what Should am I operating? *I believe I should only have to say something once.*
- What are my options? *I can continue to resent my employees, or for the next two weeks I can have my assistant remind everyone to use this new method on a daily basis. If, after one month, some people still won't comply, I can establish consequences for not signing in properly.*

2. They should behave the way I do.

Symptom: You find yourself judging any employee who does not model your exact behavior.

Solution: Be open to different ways of thinking and different ways of accomplishing any work task.

Scenario: *Cal owns a small housepainting company. He usually works as the senior painter and hires young guys to assist him. Cal has a very precise way of painting. When he paints a room, for example, he tapes all of the borders in that room before he begins. Everything—windows, doors, ceilings, and floors—is covered. Cal instructs all members of his crew to do the same thing.*

Martin recently joined Cal's crew. He's dependable, efficient, and productive, but he practices a slightly modified version of his boss's method.

Martin covers a section of the room he's painting with tape, paints that section, and then moves on to the next section.

This variation on Cal's technique drives him crazy. "Why can't you just follow my method?" he asks. "I respect your way," Martin explains, "but this method makes more sense to me. I do better work." Reluctant to jettison his best worker because of stylistic differences, Cal tries to weigh both sides of his situation:

- *What's happening here? My employee refuses to prepare a room the way I do. He tapes one section at a time, instead of covering the entire area.*
- *What his part? He insists on doing it differently.*
- *What's my part? I'm insisting he follow my technique.*
- *From what Should am I operating? He should paint my way.*
- *What are my options? I can keep insisting that he do it my way and fire him if he can't convert, or I can assess the quality of the work he does. If the section-by-section method of painting a room still produces excellent results, I can be open to different ways of accomplishing the same goal.*

3. They shouldn't make mistakes.

Symptom: You view other people's mistakes as catastrophic and unacceptable; you believe that errors are grounds for dismissal.

Solution: People who don't make mistakes aren't working. Business parents help their employees learn from their mistakes.

Scenario: *Lynn is the owner of a high-end wedding planning company. Over the past two years, she's hired five assistants. Each time she brings someone on, the relationship begins with great promise. But as soon as the assistant makes a mistake, Lynn goes overboard. "This is a high-end operation!" she yells. "We cannot afford to make mistakes." Inevitably, Lynn's employees quit.*

When Lynn interviews and hires Fontana, she believes she's finally found someone who won't let her down. Two months into the job, however, Fontana calls Lynn to confess the error she's committed. "I just real-

ized that there's a mistake on one of our wedding invitations. I must have transposed the date. I called the printer to correct the error. They can still correct the mistake and produce the job, but they have to charge an additional fee for the correction. I'm so sorry."

Lynn is furious. Her impulse is to launch into her usual rampage. At the same time, she doesn't want to lose this valuable assistant. She finds the self-restraint to bite her tongue and take an inventory:

- What's happening here? My employee just made a costly error that I'm going to have to pay for.
- What's Fontana's part? She didn't proofread the invitation carefully enough. Eventually she discovered her error and corrected it.
- What's my part? I have a very hard time forgiving her (or anyone) for making a mistake. I'm afraid it's going to cost me too much.
- From what Should am I operating? My employees shouldn't make mistakes.
- What are my options? I can deduct the cost of the corrected invitations from Fontana's salary (which could lead to her quitting), or I can consider the extra printing fee an investment in her development. We can use this accident as an opportunity. We can create office systems to reduce the likelihood of this particular problem happening again.

4. I shouldn't have to be their parent.

Symptoms: You resent having to hold people accountable for their work; you often wish that employees would just "grow up."

Solution: While this is a noble idea, it's totally unrealistic. Accept that being a manager means being a parent.

Scenario: Angelo gets hired to head up product development for the packaged cereal division of a large commercial food manufacturer. Previously, he managed product development for a much smaller cereal company. At that company, he oversaw two employees. Now he's directing a team of fifteen.

During his first week, Angelo holds a meeting with his new staff. He describes the trends he sees in the cereal industry and lays out several product ideas that he'd like his new team to investigate.

For the next two weeks, Angelo runs from meeting to meeting with the other division heads. He's immersed in learning about the corporation as a whole, its long-range plans, and its goals for each department. Meanwhile, he trusts that members of his staff are working hard on the projects he's assigned.

To his surprise, the next meeting with his staff two weeks later reveals that they've produced very little. No one has even begun to research any of the new product ideas that he suggested. Angelo can't believe the lack of initiative. "We talked about several very specific cereal concepts at our first meeting. What happened?" *he asks. One person offers,* "You weren't here, and we weren't sure exactly what you wanted us to do." *Angelo is floored. He never had this kind of problem with his tiny staff of two. In an attempt to understand his situation, he takes an inventory:*

- What's happening here? *My staff is not producing.*
- What's their part? *Two weeks ago, I gave them a list of projects I wanted started. They responded positively to the ideas but didn't pursue any of them. They seem to be waiting for me to instruct them.*
- What's my part? *I assumed that these product developers were like my old team—self-starters. I thought they would take my ideas and run with them.*
- From what Should am I operating? *I shouldn't have to be their parent.*
- What are my options? *I can resent them for being passive, or I can give my new employees more direct supervision (i.e., business parenting) by laying out exactly what I want each of them to do and tracking their progress. Over time, they will become more self-sufficient.*

5. They should know how to prioritize their work.

Symptom: You see your employees doing what you think are nonessential tasks and become infuriated.

Solution: Communicate daily what your priorities are and where you'd like your employees to focus their energies.

Scenario: *Liam manages the medical billing department for an orthopedic hospital. He has four billing clerks under his supervision. Liam is concerned because, while the clerks always look busy, they are behind in collecting money owed to the hospital. Upon closer scrutiny, Liam realizes that his staff spend the bulk of their time fielding phone calls from patients who have questions about their bills, and from vendors requesting payment.*

Liam believes that rather than answering those queries, his employees should be making calls to collect revenue from insurance companies and self-paying patients. "It seems so obvious to me," he ponders. "Why don't they understand that we can't pay our vendors or help patients unless we bring in the money that's due to us?" In an attempt to get a better grasp of his situation, Liam takes a quick accounting:

- What's happening here? *My billing department is behind in collecting revenue for the hospital because they focus so much energy responding to questions about patient bills and vendor invoices.*
- What is their part? *They're just reacting to the work that comes in rather than planning their day around collecting funds.*
- What's my part? *I keep waiting for them to wake up and take charge of the situation.*
- From what Should am I operating? *I assume that people should know how to prioritize their work.*
- What are my options? *I can set a ten-minute morning meeting, tell each clerk where to focus his or her energies for that day, and help them formulate a plan for accomplishing their priorities. I can also set up a system to help them reach their goals, such as putting certain people on the phones to answer patient questions while others make calls to collect funds.*

6. They should know what I need.

Symptom: You resent your staff for being self-centered and oblivious to your needs.

Solution: Unless you've hired mind readers, employees need to be told what you need and what you expect from them. Learn to ask for what you want.

Scenario: *Gail is the director of a fast-growing executive recruitment firm. She's preparing for an important presentation that she'll be delivering later in the day to the board of trustees of a Fortune 500 company. Gail's assistant, Mickey, keeps coming into her office with questions that interrupt her train of thought.*

On the fifth interruption, Gail explodes. "Can't you see what I'm doing here?" Mickey looks surprised and slightly puzzled. "I have one hour to prepare the most important speech for this firm, and you won't leave me alone." Mickey apologizes. "Sorry to bother you. I didn't realize . . ." As Mickey sheepishly slips out of the office, Gail realizes that she may have overreacted a bit.

Early the next day, before Mickey arrives at the office, Gail tries to review her situation:

- What's happening here? *Whenever I have an important project to complete, Mickey constantly interrupts me.*
- What's Mickey's part? *She seems oblivious to my situation and does the opposite of what is helpful.*
- What's my part? *I don't communicate what I need from Mickey because it seems so obvious.*
- From what Should am I operating? *Mickey should know what I need.*
- What are my options? *I can continue to hope that Mickey will pick up on my unspoken signals, or I can try communicating my needs more clearly. I can alert Mickey regarding my day-to-day priorities. In the future, if I have an important presentation, I can tell Mickey in advance that I need one hour of uninterrupted time.*

7. They should like and appreciate me.

Symptom: You feel hurt and excluded when employees don't treat you in a friendly manner.

Solution: If you want to be popular, join a club. Business parenting often requires a willingness to be disliked in order to do your job.

Scenario: *Anna works as the office manager for a corporate law firm. Her domain includes supervising fifteen legal secretaries who key in contracts, wills, briefs, and other legal documents all day long. One of the secretaries, Penelope, asks Anna for a lot of favors. First, Penelope has a friend in town. She begs Anna for two extra days off so that she can be a good hostess. Afraid of seeming cold or uncaring, Anna agrees. Then Penelope signs up for an acting class, and pleads with Anna to let her leave early two nights a week. "This means the world to me," she says. Again, Anna acquiesces.*

The other secretaries notice that Anna gives Penelope preferential treatment. What they aren't aware of is Anna's need to be liked. Anna is afraid to say no to Penelope's requests because she fears her secretary's disapproval.

One day, as she sits in a ladies' room stall, Anna overhears Penelope putting her down. "I can get our wimpy supervisor to do whatever I want," she brags. "She's so insecure that she'll do anything to stay on my good side." Anna is crestfallen. Still, she uses this painful situation to evaluate her own behavior.

- What's happening here? *I've been doing special favors because I was afraid Penelope wouldn't like me.*
- What's Anna's part? *She's skilled at asking for what she wants and manipulating me to say yes.*
- What's my part? *I'm too afraid of being disliked to say no to her.*
- From what Should am I operating? *The people I supervise should like me.*
- What are my options? *I can continue to try and get everyone to like me (which doesn't seem to work), or I can take a stand when necessary, say no to special favors that I don't condone, and risk not being liked.*

8. They should know that I appreciate them.

Symptom: You resent having to acknowledge, reward, or recognize your staff.

Solution: Get over it and say thank you as often as you can. Appreciation is an essential ingredient to effective management.

Scenario: *Dr. Evans takes great pride in her professional, accessible, and friendly medical practice. She sets high standards for herself and her staff. If someone makes a mistake, she's quick to correct it. Her patients constantly thank her for running such an excellent organization.*

For this reason, she's completely surprised when her office manager, Freda, leaves the following voice mail: "I'm sorry, Dr. Evans, but I can't work for you anymore. I left a letter on your desk explaining my reasons."

When Dr. Evans opens the letter, she's shocked at its contents. According to Freda, her boss never appreciates anything she does. "You always tell me when I've done something wrong, but you never acknowledge the good work that I do. I've worked for you for two years, and you've never given me a raise. You've never even said thank you for the many systems I've created to make your office run more efficiently. I can't continue to work for someone so unappreciative."

Although Freda's words stun her, the complaints strike a familiar chord. At home, Dr. Evans's children and husband often bristle at her tendency to find fault in everything they do. As she drives home from a hectic day of treating patients, she realizes that she may need to change her ways before another valuable employee quits. The next morning, as she works out with her private trainer at 6 a.m., Dr. Evans tries to diagnose her situation:

- What's happening here? *My prize employee just quit because she feels undervalued.*
- What's Freda's part? *She wanted concrete signs—words, actions, and rewards—that show her I appreciate her.*
- What's my part? *I believe that a paycheck is appreciation enough.*
- From what Should am I operating? *They should know that I appreciate them.*
- What are my options? *I can forget about Freda and look for thick-skinned employees who don't need much appreciation, or I can try practicing a few gestures of appreciation with my remaining staff. I can begin by thanking them at the end of every day, buying lunch on hectic days, and giving raises to my top performers.*

9. They should get along with one another.

Symptom: You get impatient when employees have arguments or disagreements. You view interpersonal discord as ridiculous or childish.

Solution: Business parents understand that workplace sibling rivalry is common. Figure out a way to deal with it.

Scenario: *Matt runs an urban dating service called Life in the Fast Lane. His fast-growing company provides dates for more than 3,000 single professionals. Two of his dating counselors are having trouble getting along. Louise, a longtime employee of LIFL, has bad chemistry with Judy, a new arrival.*

One Tuesday, Judy approaches Matt with her problem. "Louise isn't willing to work with me. I have candidates who could be matched up with her pool, but she refuses to discuss anything with me." Matt expresses his disbelief. "Louise is a great worker. I can't believe you two can't work together. Ask her again, and I'm sure she'll assist you." Judy persists: "You don't understand. I've tried and she won't cooperate with me." Matt waves Judy away with, "Give it another try."

One week later, Matt walks into the office to find Judy crying at her desk. "What's wrong?" he asks. "Louise contacted two of my clients and set up dates with her clients without informing me," she sniffles. "I overheard her telling one of them that she's trying to make up for my incompetence." This piece of news pushes Matt over the edge. He goes to his office and begins to assess the situation:

- *What's happening here? I have two employees who are in conflict. Louise has some prejudice against Judy and refuses to work with her.*
- *What's their part? Louise is behaving childishly. Judy doesn't know how to defend herself.*
- *What's my part? I don't want to believe that Louise could stoop to such petty behavior. I prefer thinking that Judy is exaggerating the situation.*
- *From what Should am I operating? My employees should know how to get along with each other.*

- What are my options? *I can continue to ignore the problem, or I can meet with Judy and Louise and confront their rift. I can take Louise to task about matching up candidates without the cooperation of another counselor, which is against company policy. I can insist that, from now on, Louise treat Judy with respect.*

10. They shouldn't challenge me.

Symptom: You experience suggestions, corrections, or revisions as criticism. You view the people who offer opposing opinions as insurgents.

Solution: Business parents accept challenging employees as positive contributors and teach them how to channel their suggestions in constructive ways.

Scenario: *It's the quarterly meeting to introduce the fall pant line to the sales force of a major clothing manufacturer. Larry wants to roll out the fall line and generate enthusiasm from his sales staff. He hands all of the attendees a catalog with a separate price list inside. Cally, one of the senior salespeople, raises her hand and offers a suggestion: "I think these prices could be higher. It would help improve the perceived value if you offered them for $10 more per item." Larry gets flustered, turns red, and retorts, "This is the price our market can bear. Leave the pricing to our comptroller." She persists: "No, I think you should rethink this because I could sell more at a higher—" Larry cuts her off with, "And I think you're wrong." With that he dismisses Cally and closes the meeting.*

After the meeting, Larry churns with anger. He's furious at Cally for bringing up the issue of price in front of the other salespeople. "What does she know about pricing?" He mumbles to himself. "And she's wrong."

On his way home, Larry stops off at a local retail store to check on competitive pant lines and see how their prices compare. To his chagrin, Cally is right. The company's competitors are charging at least $10 more per item for the exact same quality of garment. As Larry drives home he reconsiders his position:

- What's happening here? *One of my salespeople challenged me in a meeting regarding our prices. I didn't like her behavior. Her idea, however, has merit.*
- What's her part? *She spoke up publicly and embarrassed me.*
- What's my part? *I took her suggestion as a challenge to our comptroller. I defended the price list but later found out she was right.*
- From what Should am I operating? *Employees should not challenge me.*
- What are my options? *I can stick to my guns and keep our pant prices the same, or I can thank Cally for alerting me regarding a general pricing trend, and adjust our prices accordingly. I can request that the next time she has a suggestion, she should approach me in private.*

A Final Note

The art of managing people is an ongoing process. Each person affords a different growth opportunity for you (the business parent) and for him- or herself. Managing effectively is not easy. If you employ our techniques, they'll help you navigate the emotional minefields that are so often involved when overseeing another person's work.

MANAGING DOWN AT A GLANCE

The Four Key Principles of Business Parenting

1. **Employees need to know exactly what is expected of them.**
   Job descriptions
   Goals
   Policies and procedures

2. **Employees need consistent feedback.**
   Employee reviews
   Rewards for positive behavior
   Consequences for negative behavior

3. **Employees will test their environment.**
    Be consistent.
    Be persistent.
    Be repetitive.

4. **Business tools are a manager's best friends.**
    Use all of the above.

Nine Management Headaches

1. **The Chronically Delayed:** "My alarm didn't go off (again)."
2. **The MIA:** "I have a mysterious illness. I can't come into work."
3. **The Cynic:** "It'll never work."
4. **The Passive-Aggressive:** "I haven't done much because I don't know what you want . . ."
5. **Attention Seeker:** "Look at me! Look at me!"
6. **The Bad Attitude:** "Go get your *own* shoes."
7. **The Slug:** "I'll finish it tomorrow. I promise."
8. **The Addict:** "Mus' be zis decnjstent . . ."
9. **The Thief:** "Two paychecks? Whoops . . ."

Ten Supervisory Shoulds to Watch Out For

1. I should only have to say it once.
Accept that business parenting is an ongoing process. Repetition is part of the game. Repetition is part of the game.

2. They should behave the way I do.
Be open to different ways of thinking and different ways of accomplishing any work task.

3. They shouldn't make mistakes.
People who don't make mistakes aren't working. Business parents help their employees learn from their mistakes.

4. I shouldn't have to be their parent.
While this is a noble idea, it's totally unrealistic. Accept that being a manager means being a parent.

5. They should know how to prioritize their work.
Communicate daily what your priorities are and where you'd like your employees to focus their attention.

6. They should know what I need.
Unless you've hired mind readers, employees need to be told what you need and what you expect from them. Learn to ask for what you want.

7. They should like and appreciate me.
If you want to be popular, join a club. Business parenting often requires a willingness to be disliked in order to do your job.

8. They should know that I appreciate them.
Get over it and say thank you as often as you can. Appreciation is an essential ingredient to effective management.

9. They should get along with one another.
Business parents understand that workplace sibling rivalry is common. Figure out a way to manage.

10. They shouldn't challenge me.
Business parents accept challenging employees as positive contributors and teach them how to channel their suggestions in constructive ways.

8

Corporate Culture—Is This the Right Place for You?

New Recruits to Disney Theme Parks attend Disney University,
where they are introduced to a new language and become
indoctrinated in the Disney way of doing things:
Employees are "cast members." Customers are "guests."
A work shift is "a performance." Employees learn Disney
slogans such as "Even if it's a rough day, we appear happy."
"You've got to have an honest smile that comes from within."
Facial hair on men, heavy makeup on women,
and cursing of any kind are not allowed.
—*from* Built to Last, *by James C. Collins and Jerry I. Porras*

Up to this point, we've focused on the skill of unhooking from confining roles, toxic relationships, Boundary Busters, and emotionally charged situations at work. We've argued that if you can change your reaction to external conditions, you can change (and improve) the quality of your daily experience in the workplace. But what happens when you've unhooked in every way imaginable and you still feel unhappy at work? What options are available to you then?

In certain cases, you may master the art of unhooking and still suffer from recurring feelings of frustration, anger, helplessness, anxiety, or despair on the job. In those situations, the emotional discomfort you experience may have less to do with the particular people and circumstances than with the company itself. Sometimes your personality, your ethics, and your way of doing business may clash with your employer's culture.

Every company has a culture. Some cultures are more clearly defined than others. **Corporate culture** is a term that describes the predominant attitudes, behaviors, values and ethics practiced within an organization. Through our work with hundreds of companies and thousands of individuals, we've seen one very consistent theme: *Long-term job satisfaction is directly influenced by how well your personal attitudes, behaviors, values, and ethics match those of your employer.* In other words, if you don't like to smile, you won't like working at Disneyland.

The ability to uncover a company's culture is critical because, once it is exposed, you can understand how it is affecting you. For example, if you discover that you're working in a highly political environment where posturing and self-promotion are rewarded, and yet you thrive in settings where direct communication and mutual support are the rule, you'll finally comprehend why you feel so uneasy on the job. Or if you realize that your employer expects you to be available 24/7 for company business, and you're determined to spend quality time with your kids, you'll know why you feel intensely conflicted every time a work obligation interferes with family time.

Unfortunately, most cultures aren't as easily discernible as Disney's. Frequently, employees interpret a bad cultural fit as "there must be something wrong with *me*."

- *Take Robert, a low-key guy in a high-stakes environment. He works for a brokerage firm where quick decision-making, competition between coworkers, and risk-taking is rewarded. Robert is extremely talented at analyzing long-range market trends, but he doesn't move fast enough on the trading floor to convert his analyses into profits. "Next to the other traders, I'm a snail," he confides. "I'm not aggressive enough to make a real killing."*

- *Then there's Gwen, the director of marketing for an established national symphony. She spends most of her time responding to interoffice e-mail and attending lengthy meetings. A natural pioneer, Gwen gets tired of "decision-making by committee." Lately, she finds herself snapping at coworkers. "I love the symphony, but I hate the bureaucracy. Any marketing initiative I introduce takes months to become a watered-down version of the original idea." The symphony's interdepartmental politics zap Gwen's energy. "I've lost any of the excitement I once had for my job."*

- *Alicia is a veteran TV news producer. Initially, she couldn't wait to produce stories for top network news shows. Her segments on social issues have won numerous journalism and television awards. Now, fifteen years later, Alicia is singing a different tune: "I'm tired of running around. I've had it with working under extreme time deadlines and I'm sick of dealing with volatile television personalities." While she complains about the conditions of her work environment, Alicia secretly fears that her dissatisfaction might really mean she's lost her creative edge.*

Each of these individuals feels unhappy and frustrated at work. Each person is experiencing prolonged discomfort on the job. While you might argue that Robert needs to learn how to trade faster, Gwen should buck up and deal with the bureaucracy, and Alicia ought to adjust her attitude, we propose that the real issue in each case is a culture clash. None of these people currently inhabit a work environment that is a "good fit." In Alicia's case, she's outgrown the very setting she used to love.

Know Yourself, Know Your Company

Here we offer you the opportunity to investigate your employer's culture and determine how well it suits you. By taking our corporate culture assessment, you can clarify your own attitudes, behaviors, values, and ethics and compare them to those of your workplace. While taking the assessment, you may discover that small things like dress code and physical environment really do matter to you.

You may also realize what the details of your work environment reveal about the company as a whole.

The Corporate Culture Assessment

The corporate culture assessment begins with a personal inventory. You'll be reading and responding to sixteen questions that cover a broad range of workplace issues. Carefully consider your answer to each question. The personal inventory will give you a clearer picture of the best work environment for you.

Personal Inventory

1. At this time in your career, what kind of general work environment do you want? (Circle one.)

   A. Friendly, collegial—team approach, success is shared.
   B. Competitive, win/lose—concrete rewards for high performance.
   C. Conformist—steady rewards if you play by the rules.
   D. Political—become an ally with those in power and navigate up.
   E. Creative, individualistic—make your mark with original ideas.
   F. Other _____

2. What kind of dress code do you most prefer? (Circle one.)

   A. Classic corporate
   B. Relaxed professional
   C. Fashion forward
   D. Alternative—originality counts
   E. Casual
   F. Uniform required
   G. Other _____

3. Which of the following approaches to work fits you best? (Circle one.)

A. Hard drive—overachieving is the norm; work hard to move ahead. Long hours are part of the game. Building your career is the highest priority.
B. Low gear—things move slowly but predictably. It's a day job.
C. Change the world—commit time and energy to a noble cause. Make a difference in other people's lives.
D. Middle of the road—work is engaging but not consuming. There is a ladder to climb but you also have time for your personal life.
E. Mom-and-pop—perform a variety of tasks in a small, cozy environment. Be part of the company family.
F. Status—image counts. Work for established name in an attractive environment. Being associated with a reputable company is key.

4. **Rate all of the following qualities in their order of importance to you at work** (1 = extremely important, 5 = not important at all):

Creativity   _____
Efficiency   _____
Fairness   _____
Honesty   _____
Innovation   _____
Kindness   _____
Power   _____
Prestige   _____
Profitability   _____
Respect   _____
Responsibility   _____
Status   _____
Tradition   _____

5. **Rate all of the following rewards in order of importance to you** (1 = extremely important, 5 = not important at all):

_____ Financial rewards

_____ Public recognition—acknowledgment for achievement

_____ Promotion—new title, more responsibility

_____ Benefits—education, travel, vacation time, pension plans, health coverage

_____ Flexible hours—time for self and family

_____ Social value—making a contribution to society

_____ Creative license—freedom to express ideas

6. **Which management style are you most comfortable with?** (Circle one.)

A. Structured—management sets the goals and monitors performance.
B. Loose—you can do what you want but you have to show results.
C. Hands-on—everything you do is watched and carefully monitored daily.
D. Team approach—work as a team and get rewarded as a team.
E. Free-for-all—no guidelines or accountability, management distracted.
F. Other _____

7. **Which of these do you believe an individual should be promoted for?** (Circle the ones you agree with.)

A. Achievement—exceeding expectations
B. Innovation—generating fresh ideas
C. Masterful political maneuvering
D. Having the right connections
E. Sacrifice and hard work
F. Good looks
G. Other _____

8. **What communication style do you prefer in a company?**

   A. Direct communication—I like to be kept informed about everything through meetings, e-mails, and voice mail.
   B. Chain of command—communication is filtered and delivered to those who need to know.
   C. Informal—news travels through word of mouth.
   D. I'm only interested in the information that pertains to me.
   E. Don't ask, don't tell—communication is overrated.
   F. Other _____

9. **Which decision-making style works best for you?** (Circle one.)

   A. Company encourages employees to make decisions at all levels.
   B. Decisions are made by a committee made up of representatives from every department.
   C. Decisions are made by consensus; everyone affected must agree.
   D. Authorities make decisions and pass their decisions down to others.
   E. Other _____

10. **When a crisis occurs, which approach are you most comfortable with?** (Circle one.)

   A. Work together as a team to solve the crisis.
   B. Find out who is responsible and have his or her team clean it up.
   C. Find out who is responsible and make the individual clean it up.
   D. Cover up the crisis and deal with it behind closed doors.
   E. Ignore the problem. Things tend to work themselves out.
   F. Other _____

11. **When an employee is caught breaking a company rule, what should be done?** (Circle one.)

A. Immediate dismissal
B. Warning, followed by close monitoring
C. Informal reprimand by direct supervisor
D. Isolate and humiliate
E. No consequences
F. Other _____

12. **How do you expect to feel at work?** (Circle one.)

A. Happy and content.
B. Frustrated but gratified because I'm making a difference.
C. Grateful to have a job—never mind if it's a little boring.
D. Skeptical—work is not about feeling good; it's about getting paid.
E. Angry and resentful—work is a pain in my _____ .
F. Successful and encouraged.
G. Other _____

13. **In your opinion, which of these qualities should it take to get ahead?** (Circle all that you feel are important.)

A. Hard worker
B. Innovator
C. Politician
D. Plays by the rules
E. Gets along with everyone
F. Income producer
G. Other _____

14. **How would you rate your ability to deal effectively with company politics?**

A. Extremely high
B. High
C. Average
D. Low
E. No ability at all

15. **How much stress are you willing to have in your work life?**

    A. Espresso
    B. Strong coffee
    C. Regular cup of coffee
    D. Decaffeinated
    E. Herbal tea

16. **Which phrase best describes your overall moral code at work?**

    A. Be honest and honorable.
    B. Do well when you can. When you can't, make money.
    C. Don't ask, don't tell.
    D. The truth is relative.
    E. Survival of the fittest.
    F. Other _____

Now that you've completed the personal inventory, you can move on to the workplace appraisal. To accurately evaluate the culture of the company, we ask you to read and provide answers to the following questions. To render an accurate appraisal of your workplace culture, do your best to look beyond the *stated* company values, and identify the behaviors and attitudes that are *actually* rewarded.

Workplace Appraisal

1. **How would you describe your company's general work environment?** (Circle one.)

    A. Friendly, collegial—team approach, success is shared.
    B. Competitive, win/lose—concrete rewards for high performance.
    C. Conformist—steady rewards if you play by the rules.
    D. Political—become an ally with those in power and navigate up.
    E. Creative, individualistic—make your mark with original ideas.
    F. Other _____

2. **What is the dress code?** (Circle one.)
   A. Classic corporate
   B. Relaxed professional
   C. Fashion forward
   D. Alternative—originality counts
   E. Casual
   F. Uniform required
   G. Other _____

3. **Which of the following best describes your employer's approach to work?** (Circle one.)
   A. Hard drive—overachieving is the norm; we all work hard to move ahead and create results. We put in overtime regularly.
   B. Low gear—things here move slowly but predictably. We complete our work shifts and go home.
   C. Change the world—we all commit time and energy to making a difference. We sacrifice for a noble cause.
   D. Middle of the road—we aim for reasonable productivity. Work should be engaging but not consuming. We allow time for your personal life.
   E. Mom-and-pop—everyone is expected to perform a variety of tasks in a small, cozy environment. We treat you like family.
   F. Status—image counts. We work for established name in an attractive environment. We all look good and reflect the status of our company.

4. **Rate all of the following qualities in order of their value within the company.** *Hint: Valued qualities are often rewarded through promotions, pay raises, public recognition, etc.* (1 = valued very highly, 5 = not valued at all)

   Creativity   _____
   Efficiency   _____
   Fairness   _____
   Honesty   _____

Innovation   _____
Kindness   _____
Power   _____
Prestige   _____
Profitability   _____
Respect   _____
Responsibility   _____
Status   _____
Tradition   _____

5. **Based on your experience, what kinds of rewards are available in your company? Rate all of the following rewards in order of importance in your company** (1 = extremely important, 5 = not important at all):

_____ Financial rewards

_____ Public recognition—acknowledgment for achievement

_____ Promotion—new title, more responsibility

_____ Benefits—education, travel, vacation time, pension plans, health coverage

_____ Flexible hours—time for self and family

_____ Social value—making a contribution to society

_____ Creative license—freedom to express ideas

6. **What would you say is the management style of your company?** (Circle one.)

A. Structured—management sets the goals and monitors your performance.
B. Loose—you can do what you want but you have to show results.
C. Micromanagement—everything you do is critiqued and revised.

D. Team approach—work as a team, get rewarded as a team.

E. Absentee—no guidelines, no accountability.

F. Other _____

7. **In your opinion, what are promotions based on?** (Circle the ones that pertain.)

A. Achievement

B. Innovation

C. Political maneuvering

D. Having the right connections

E. Sacrifice and hard work

F. Good looks

G. Other _____

8. **Which phrase best describes your company's communication style?** (Circle one.)

A. Direct communication—through meetings, e-mails, and voice mail.

B. Chain of command—information filters down through the ranks.

C. Hearsay—sometimes you hear it, sometimes you don't.

D. Smoke signals—random vague messages that you are left to interpret.

E. What communication?

F. Other _____

9. **In your experience, how are decisions made in the company?** (Circle one.)

A. By individuals at all levels within the company.

B. By committee—someone from every department participates.

C. By consensus—everyone affected must agree.

D. By authorities who pass their decisions down to others.

E. Other _____

10. What is the company approach when a crisis arises? (Circle one.)

   A. Work together as a team to solve the crisis.

   B. Find out who is responsible and have that person's team clean it up.

   C. Find someone to blame and make that person the scapegoat.

   D. Cover up the crisis; deal with it behind closed doors.

   E. Deny the crisis until it becomes unmanageable.

   F. Other _____

11. What are the consequences for misconduct in the company? (Circle one.)

   A. Immediate dismissal

   B. Warning, followed by close monitoring

   C. Informal reprimand by direct supervisor

   D. Isolate and humiliate

   E. No consequences

   F. Other _____

12. How would you best describe the way employees feel at work? (Circle one.)

   A. Happy and content.

   B. They are frustrated at times, but feel good about their contribution.

   C. Grateful to have a job—never mind if it's a little boring.

   D. Skeptical—work is not about feeling good; it's about getting paid.

   E. Angry and resentful.

   F. Successful and encouraged.

   G. Other _____

13. What kind of person does best in this company? (Circle one.)

   A. Hard worker

   B. Innovator

   C. Politician

D. Rule keeper—learns and plays by the rules
E. Collegial—able to get along with everyone
F. Rainmaker—makes money for the company
G. Other _____

14. **How would you rate the level of politics in your company?** (Circle one.)

A. Extremely high
B. High
C. Average
D. Low
E. Other _____

15. **How would you rate the level of stress in your company?** (Circle one.)

A. Espresso
B. Strong coffee
C. Regular cup of coffee
D. Decaffeinated
E. Other _____

16. **Which phrase best describes the overall value system of your company?** (Circle one.)

A. Be honest and honorable.
B. Do well when you can. When you can't, make money.
C. Don't ask, don't tell.
D. The truth is relative.
E. Survival of the fittest.
F. Other _____

The third and final part of the corporate culture assessment is a comparison grid. By taking your answers to the personal inventory and juxtaposing them to your responses to the workplace appraisal, you can literally see where you stand in relation to your company.

Remember Gwen? She's trying to understand why she feels so confined and frustrated as the director of marketing for a prominent national symphony. Her comparison grid sheds valuable light on the ways in which her personal values and work style clash with the symphony.

Corporate Culture Comparison Grid

Name: Gwen

Position: Director of Marketing, ABC Symphony

1. General work environment I want	1. General work environment I'm in
Creative, individualistic	Political

2. Dress code I prefer	2. Company's dress code
Relaxed professional	Classic corporate

3. Best approach to work for me	3. Company's approach to work
Middle of the road	Middle of the road

4. Qualities I value on the job   4. Qualities the company values

	I value	Company values
Creativity	1	5
Efficiency	3	1
Fairness	3	5
Honesty	1	4
Innovation	1	4
Kindness	2	5
Power	5	2
Prestige	5	1
Profitability	5	1
Respect	5	2
Responsibility	3	1
Status	3	2
Tradition	3	1

5. **Rewards I want**

		5. **Rewards the company gives**
Financial rewards	1	5
Public recognition	5	1
Promotion	5	1
Benefits	3	1
Flexible hours	5	3
Social value	1	1
Creative license	1	5

6. **Management style I prefer**

Loose—you can do what you want but you have to show results.

6. **Company's management style**

Micromanagement—everything you do is critiqued and revised.

7. **My reasons for promotion**

Achievement, Innovation

7. **Company's reasons for promotion**

Political manuevering, Sacrifice

8. **My communication style**

Direct

8. **Company's communication style**

Smoke signals

9. **Decision-making I prefer**

Company encourages employees to make decisions at all levels.

9. **Company's decision-making**

Authorities make decisions and pass their decisions down to others.

10. **My approach to crisis**

Work together as a team to solve the crisis.

10. **Company's approach to crisis**

Cover up the crisis and deal with it behind closed doors.

11. Consequences for misconduct	11. Consequences for misconduct
Informal reprimand by	Isolate and humiliate
direct supervisor	

12. How I expect to feel	12. How employees feel
Successful and encouraged	Angry and resentful

13. Who should get ahead (top 3)	13. Who gets ahead (top 3)
Hard worker	Hard worker
Gets along with everyone	Politician
Innovator	Income producer

14. Level of politics I prefer	14. Level of politics at work
Average	High

15. Preferred stress level	15. Level of stress at work
Regular cup of coffee	Espresso

16. My value system	16. Company moral code
Honest and honorable	Survival of the fittest

As Gwen's chart indicates, she's in a work environment that runs contrary to her nature. Her corporate culture assessment illuminates why the endless meetings and bureaucratic red tape at ABC Symphony bring her down. At the same time, Gwen can appreciate the fact that her job doesn't consume all of her time. As question number three indicates, she prefers a job that affords time for her personal life.

Your Corporate Culture Comparison Grid

Now it's your turn. Combine your responses on the personal inventory with your answers to the workplace appraisal to see how well your company's culture fits your attitudes, behavior, values, and ethics.

Name: _____

Position: _____

1. General work environment I want	1. General work environment I'm in
_____	_____
2. Dress code I prefer	2. Company's dress code
_____	_____
3. Best approach to work for me	3. Company's approach to work
_____	_____
4. Qualities I value on the job (rate 1–5)	4. Qualities the company values (rate 1–5)

Creativity	_____	_____
Efficiency	_____	_____
Fairness	_____	_____
Honesty	_____	_____
Innovation	_____	_____
Kindness	_____	_____
Power	_____	_____
Prestige	_____	_____
Profitability	_____	_____
Respect	_____	_____
Responsibility	_____	_____
Status	_____	_____
Tradition	_____	_____

5. Rewards I want (rate 1–5)	5. Rewards the company gives (rate 1–5)

Financial rewards	_____	_____
Public recognition	_____	_____
Promotion	_____	_____
Benefits	_____	_____

Flexible hours   _____   _____
Social value   _____   _____
Creative license   _____   _____

6. Management style I prefer   6. Company's management style

_____   _____

_____   _____

_____   _____

7. My reasons for promotion   7. Company's reasons for
   (top 2)   promotion (top 2)

_____   _____

_____   _____

8. My communication style   8. Company's communication
                                        style

_____   _____

9. Decision-making I prefer   9. Company's decision-making

_____   _____

_____   _____

10. My approach to crisis   10. Company's approach to crisis

_____   _____

_____   _____

11. Consequences for   11. Consequences for
    misconduct   misconduct

_____   _____

_____   _____

12. How I expect to feel   12. How employees feel

_____   _____

13. Who should get ahead (top 3)

_____

_____

_____

13. Who gets ahead (top 3)

_____

_____

_____

14. Level of politics I prefer

_____

14. Level of politics at work

_____

15. Preferred stress level

_____

15. Level of stress at work

_____

16. My moral code at work

_____

16. General value system at work

_____

After the Assessment

Now that you've completed your assessment, here's how you can use the information to empower yourself at work. Pay careful attention to questions four and five. Notice when the qualities and rewards that you want differ greatly from the qualities and rewards that your company offers.

If your company's culture generally matches your personal inventory, you can trust that you're in a work environment that suits you. Equipped with this information, you can focus your energy on operating most effectively within the culture. In this case, unhooking techniques will help you navigate any interpersonal snags that you encounter within the organization.

If it's a mismatch; if the culture runs contrary to your ethics, values, and business practices, you can search for a better fit. This could mean:

A. Finding a new job at a new company with ethics, morals, and business practices closer to yours.
B. Finding a new job in the same company working for a boss whose value system is closer to yours.
C. Staying put, but keeping an eye out for opportunities A and B.

How Companies Change Cultures

The company you presently work for may be very different from the one that first hired you. This is because *cultures change as leadership changes*. There are two events that usually lead to a corporate culture overhaul:

1. When a company merges with or is sold to another company with a different culture.
2. When a company changes management—current leadership leaves or retires.

If you work at a company that's undergone a change in leadership or ownership, and you long for the way things used to be, it's probably due to the fact that you're working in an environment where the ethics, values, and business practices have changed. This new set of rules may go against your personal value system. The following are two case studies where structural changes led to cultural changes.

The Merger

Ralph is a lifetime employee of Homestead Bank, an institution that takes pride in practicing family values. He and most of his colleagues have worked there for more than fifteen years. They feel a sense of loyalty and commitment to their customers and to the community. The bank has a reputation for looking after its employees. It offers flextime so that employees can attend their children's school conferences or accompany their elderly parents to medical appointments.

One year ago, Homestead Bank merged with a much larger commercial bank. This larger bank is more competitive and more profit-oriented. Employees are expected to work longer hours. There is no flextime. All medical and school appointments must be scheduled after work. If a family emergency arises, you have to take the time off as a sick day, personal day, or vacation day.

Ralph has an elderly father who's taken ill. They live in the same town. As long as he worked for Homestead Bank, Ralph could take off a couple of hours to accompany his father to the hospital or to a doctor's appointment, return to work within two hours, and make the time up later in the week. Now he must either take the whole day off or pay a nurse's aid to escort his father.

Ralph's father has a degenerative illness. By the end of the first year, Ralph has used up all of his sick days and vacation days. Whereas in the old culture, he'd want to give the bank double time for every hour he took off, now he feels resentful for the lack of generosity on the part of his employer. He longs for the old company.

After Ralph takes the corporate culture assessment, he realizes that the bank's culture has changed dramatically over the past year. Faced with the fact that he strongly dislikes the new culture, Ralph must make a decision. Either he adjusts to the new culture or he looks for a new job. Because he needs the secure paycheck, Ralph isn't ready to move at this time. Still, he can begin to investigate other job opportunities with companies that come closer to his value system.

A Change in Management

Kate works as a sound engineer for a music production company. Her company records and distributes the latest in country-and-western music. Kate joined this growing corporation five years ago. At that time, it was a fledgling enterprise. The founder, Earl, is a charismatic entrepreneur who encouraged forward thinking and breakthrough ideas. His conference room looked more like a living room. It had armchairs, couches, musical instruments, and a large bowl of M&M's in the middle of a guitar-shaped coffee table. You could put your feet up, pitch new talent or discuss current projects, and enjoy the camaraderie of your coworkers.

Last summer, Earl retired. His replacement is a businessman from Chicago named Sterling. This new leader is more corporate. One of the first things Sterling did was to convert the living room into a conference room. Now Kate finds herself sitting in a straight-backed chair around a large conference table with notepads at each person's station. Instead of bowls of M&M's

with a free-for-all approach to contributing new ideas, it's Danish and filtered opinions.

Sterling likes to give PowerPoint presentations graphing profit earnings for each quarter. His favorite words all start with P—productivity, profitability, procedures, policies, permission, and protocol. His new hires all have MBAs or degrees in accounting.

Kate doesn't recognize her former company. She misses the days when everyone pitched in to complete recording projects and you never knew what the next day would bring. While she understands that the company may benefit from this more structured approach to growing a business, she's not sure if the culture fits her anymore. Does she want to work for this more mature company or is it time to go?

Kate takes the corporate cultural assessment. As she reviews the comparison grid, it becomes very clear that the new management does not fit her entrepreneurial style. She must accept that with Earl's departure, the company that used to be her second home is now a foreign land. Over time, she decides to join forces with her coworkers and start another recording studio.

Uncover a Company's Culture *Before* You Take the Job

The next time you're searching for a new job, make it your mission to uncover the company's culture before accepting any position. Why? Because, if the culture is a good fit, the likelihood that you'll enjoy your new job will increase tenfold. At the same time, if it's a bad fit, you'll have the option of dodging a career bullet.

1. Learn to identify the culture the minute you walk in.

As you walk into the company environment, notice how it looks and feels. Whatever reactions you have, heed them. Early impressions are frequently accurate.

- **Notice the physical environment**—Is it clean or dirty, organized or chaotic? Are the offices furnished or unfurnished, designed or thrown together? Is the building or physical space dark and dingy or bright and fresh? Does the overall facility communicate prosperity or deprivation?

- **Tune in to the attitude emanating from employees**—Do the company's employees seem energetic or sluggish? Does the pace feel hectic or relaxed? As you walk in, are you greeted in a friendly manner? Does the general atmosphere feel warm or cold, hip or stodgy? Do you pick up an attitude of fun and creativity, or tradition and conservatism? Does it feel collegial or competitive?

2. Uncover the culture during the interview process.

As you converse with your potential employer, look for subtle signs about the company. Be ready to ask questions that will reveal different aspects of the culture. Here are some examples:

- What are the company's hours?
- What hours do you (the interviewer) keep?
- What are the hours of the department I'll be working for?
- How long have you (the interviewer) been with the company?
- How long has the person I will be working for been here?
- How are decisions made—and how are those decisions communicated to staff?
- What role does the person who gets this position play in decision-making?

As you speak to the interviewer, look for that person's stress level. Does he or she seem harried or at ease? Does the person seem generally satisfied or frustrated with his or her own job? What kind of attire is the interviewer wearing? How does he or she interact with other members of the staff?

3. After the interview, do your homework.

The best way to decipher a culture is to speak directly with the people who've worked in it. For this reason, it always benefits you to make contact with both current and former employees. Though it may be difficult to track down these individuals, it's worth the effort.

- Meet or speak with potential coworkers to get a better idea of the culture.
- Meet or speak with the person you are replacing if possible.
- Meet or speak with past employees of the company.

Questions to ask past or present employees:

1. Can you give me three brief phrases that describe your company?
2. What do you now know about your company that you wish you had known coming in?
3. How do employees get promoted?
4. How is appreciation shown to employees?
5. What behaviors are rewarded?
6. What behaviors are frowned upon?
7. Do you always know what is expected of you?

You may feel uncomfortable asking some of these questions. That's okay. We encourage you to pose as many questions as you can to unearth cultural information about your potential employer. The important point is to actively investigate the values, ethics, and business practices of a company before you sign on as a member of the staff.

A Case Study

Elizabeth is an estate lawyer who left her last job when she had her first baby. After a year of full-time mothering, she's ready to return to the workplace. Her needs, however, have changed now that she has a child at home. She's looking for a job where she can have a more balanced life.

The first job listing that Elizabeth answers calls her back. It's a reputable estate law firm, and they want her to come in for an interview. While she knows that her potential employer will be looking at her, she's determined to scrutinize them as well. She wants to uncover the culture before taking the job.

1. Learn to identify the culture the minute you walk in.

Physical environment: Elizabeth notices that the office is really beautiful. Architecturally, it feels open and clean. The rooms are thoughtfully decorated with classic furniture and fine art. She's impressed.

Attitude emanating from the employees: Elizabeth observes that while the space is very attractive, the employees seem harried and stressed out. Their demeanor is friendly, but they appear to be moving at a very rapid pace.

2. Uncover the culture during the interview process.

Elizabeth is interviewed by a panel of three: a senior partner, a junior partner, and the head of human resources. She answers their questions easily, and enjoys the notion of going back into estate law. As the interview winds down, Elizabeth asks a few questions of her own.

"I'd like to know what the company hours are," she begins. The HR person replies, "General office hours are 8 a.m. to 6 p.m." Elizabeth looks over at the junior partner and asks him, "What hours do you keep?" He replies, "I'm never out of here before 8 p.m." Because she'll be working for the senior partner, Elizabeth poses this question: "What are the hours of your department?" He smiles and says, "As long as you get your work done, you can leave whenever you want." At that, the junior partner lets out an uneasy laugh.

Elizabeth wraps up her interview by asking each of the firm members how long they've been with the company. She learns that the human resources person has been there one year. The junior partner signed on three years ago, and the senior partner founded the firm fifteen years ago.

3. Do your homework after the interview.

Elizabeth leaves the interview interested in the job yet not really knowing what the hours of her new position would be. She decides to review the firm's Web site to see if there's anyone on staff that she knows. To her delight, she spots a lawyer with whom she went to law school. She calls him the next day and asks if he'd be willing to meet for coffee.

Over cappuccinos, Elizabeth and her former classmate catch up socially for a few minutes. Then Elizabeth begins her research regarding the firm. "What three phrases best describe your company?" she asks. "Stress, long hours, and more stress," he responds. "What do you now know about this law firm that you wish you'd known coming in?" Elizabeth asks. "Our senior partners are all maniacs," he confides. "They live, breathe, and eat work. They expect you to do the same."

At that point, Elizabeth has obtained the crucial piece of information she needs to decide about the job. Clearly, this company's culture will not allow her to live a balanced life. It does not fit her needs as a young mother. She thanks her colleague for his time, and he runs back to the office.

The world of work is one of constant flux. Companies open, close, change management, merge, and reinvent themselves. The responsibility lies with you to determine the kind of environment you want to work in and the type of culture where you can best perform. Use the corporate culture assessment to gain a clearer understanding of what you require to have a fulfilling work experience. Then decide how much you are willing to compromise.

CORPORATE CULTURE AT A GLANCE

Assess Your Company's Culture to See If It Fits You in Terms of . . .

- General work environment
- Dress code
- Attitude toward work
- Reward system
- Management style
- Reasons for promotion
- Communication style
- Decision-making
- Crisis management
- Consequences for misconduct
- Employee morale
- Level of politics
- Stress level
- Moral code

Cultures Change When . . .

1. One company merges with or is sold to another company.
2. There's a change in management—current leadership leaves or retires.

Uncover a Company's Culture Before You Take the Job

1. Begin to identify the culture the minute you walk in:
   - Notice the physical environment.
   - Tune in to the attitude emanating from employees.

2. Uncover the culture during the interview process.

3. After the interview, do your homework:
   - Interview current and/or past employees.

Index

A

Absentee boss, 128, 145–46, 155
absenteeism (employee), 59, 163, 166–68
addiction (employee), 164, 176–78
agenda for meetings
  as documentation, with notes, 111
  inclusive nature of, 110
  managing up and coming to every meeting with a detailed agenda, 110–11, 117, 125
  prioritizing problems and questions, 110
  sample, 111
appointments
  anticipating and solving problems concerning, 115
  clarifying logistics, 114
  confirming, 114
  passive-aggressive employee and "forgetting" to confirm, 164
  setting, with boss, 108–10, 117
Attention Seeker-type employee, 164, 172–73
Avoider-type boss, 128, 129–31, 154

B

Bad Attitude-type employee, 164, 173–75
boss (problems with), xii, xiv, xvi, xvii, 2, 127–55

the Absentee, 128, 145–46, 155
the Avoider, 128, 129–31, 154
as Boundary Buster, 30–31, 36–37
Charming Cheating Liar (CCL), 128, 137–39, 154
the Controlling Egomaniac, 128, 141–45, 155
the Credit Stealer, 128, 151–54, 155
difficult bosses, 127–28, 129–39, 154
emotional reactions to, 14, 105, 127
Exploder, 73, 74–75, 76–77, 83, 90–92, 99, 100
Exploder, unhooking from, 91–92
extreme bosses, 128–29, 139–55
four D's for unhooking (detect, detach, depersonalize, deal), 141, 155
getting unhooked from conflicts with, 15–17, 129–39, 141
managing up to solve problems with, 103–26 (*see also* managing up)
oversteps personal information boundary, 36–37
Pedestal Smasher, 73, 80–81, 83, 96–97, 99, 101
poor managers, reasons for, 105–6
the Sacred Cow, 128, 134–37, 154

boss *(continued)*
  seven stages of a Fatal Attraction
    at work, 140
  the Shoot-the-Messenger, 128,
    131–34, 154
  "terrible," 104–5
  trading favors with, 138, 139
  the Unpleasant, 128, 148–51,
    155
  See also managing up
boundaries (workplace), xvi, 23–46
  basics of setting, 46
  Boundary Busters, xvi, 30–31,
    36–37
  cell phones and, 45
  coworker overstepping
    interpersonal boundary,
    example, 23–24, 33–34, 44
  differing interpersonal boundaries,
    24–25
  e-mail and, 45
  emotional expression and, xii,
    28–29, 37–39, 46
  food and, 45
  guidelines, 23, 42–43
  identifying as a problem, 31
  interpersonal boundaries, 25
  keeping one's word and, 27–28,
    34–36, 46
  language and, 45
  manners/courtesy and, 29–30,
    39–40, 44, 46
  noise and, xii, 30, 40–42, 46
  partially successful results, 44
  personal hygiene and, 45
  personal information and, xii,
    28, 36–37, 46
  personal space and, xii, 26–27,
    33–34, 46
  physical contact and, 27
  smells and, 45
  successful results, 43–44
  time and, xii, 26, 32–33, 46
  unhooking process, 31, 46

  unsuccessful boundary setting,
    44
  See also time issues
breath, focusing on, 5, 6, 7, 41, 91,
  93
"count to six" method, 6, 98–99
Built to Last (Collins and Porras),
  194
business toolbox, 10–13, 17
  agenda of meetings, with notes,
    12, 111
  disciplinary action forms, 12
  documenting, 10, 12–13, 19, 36,
    40, 95–96, 131, 168, 171–72,
    173, 178
  employee benchmarks/goals, 11,
    97, 158–59, 162
  follow-up report, 92
  job descriptions, 10, 11, 93, 158,
    162, 163
  managing down (business
    parenting), use of, 162–63
  memos, e-mails, letters, 12, 33,
    34, 37
  performance reviews, 10, 12,
    160, 162, 170
  performance standards, 10
  policies and procedures (P&P)
    manual or handbook, 12, 39,
    159–60, 162, 166 (*see also*
    policies and procedures
    [P&P] manual)
  staff meetings, 162, 163, 174
    (*see also* meetings)
  status reports, 115–16, 117, 125,
    134
  write-ups and warnings, 162, 169

C
Caregiver role, 48, 50–51, 77–78
  unhooking from, 58–59, 70
cell phones, use of, 45
Charming Cheating Liar (CCL)-
  type boss, 128, 137–39, 154

Chip on the Shoulder employee,
73, 82–83, 84, 97–99, 102
  unhooking from, 98–99
Collins, James C., 194
communication styles (company),
200, 205, 209, 212
confidentiality, 122–23, 126
Controlling Egomaniac boss, 128,
141–45, 155
corporate culture, 195, 221
  bad fit with, 195–96
  case study in determining
    employee-company fit,
    218–20
  communication style, 200, 205,
    209, 212
  company rule enforcement,
    200–201, 206, 210, 212
  crisis management, 200, 206,
    209, 212
  decision-making style, 200,
    205–6, 209, 212
  dress code, 197, 203, 208, 211
  employee attitude toward work,
    201, 210, 212, 217, 219
  employer's approach to work, 203
  general work environment, 197,
    202, 208, 211, 216–17, 219
  how cultures change, 214, 221
  identifying corporate cultures
    (quickly), 216–20, 221
  individual working style, 197–98,
    206–7, 208, 211
  interview process, questions to
    ask past or present employees,
    218, 220
  interview process, questions to
    ask potential employer, 217,
    219
  long-term job satisfaction and, 195
  management change, and
    change in culture, 215–16
  management style, 199, 204–5,
    209, 212

  mergers and change in culture,
    214–15
  moral code or value system, 202,
    207, 210, 213
  politics, 201, 207, 210, 213
  promotions, basis of, 199, 205,
    209, 212
  qualities for advancement in,
    201, 209, 213
  qualities prized by employees or
    company, 198, 203–4, 208,
    211
  rewards of, 198–99, 204, 209,
    211–12
  stress level, 202, 207, 210, 213
corporate culture assessment
  comparison grid, 208–13
  personal inventory, 197–202
  putting the information to work,
    213
  using the information, 213
  workplace appraisal, 202–207
coworker
  as Boundary Buster, 30
  as Empty Pit, 73, 77–78, 92–94,
    99, 100
  facing an attitude in, 8–9
  as irritant, xii, 14
  not keeping his word, 34–36
  overstepping interpersonal
    boundary, example, 23–24,
    33–34, 43–44
  Saboteur, 73, 78–80, 83, 94–96,
    99, 101
  setting manners and courtesy
    boundaries, 39–40, 44
  setting a noise boundary, 40–42
Credit Stealer boss, 128, 151–54,
  155
crisis management, 200, 206, 209,
  212
customer
  as Boundary Buster, 30, 32–33
  as irritant, xii, 1–2

customer *(continued)*
  physical symptoms of being
    hooked, 13
  time boundary problem
    (customer misses deadlines),
    32–33, 43
Cynic-type employee, 164, 168–70

D
decision-making style, 200, 205–6,
  209
department operations as irritant,
  xii
dress code, 159, 160, 196, 197, 203,
  208, 211

E
e-mail in the workplace
  documentation through, 12, 33,
    34, 37
  unsolicited or annoying, 45
emotional expression in the
  workplace, xii, 28–29, 37–39,
  46
emotional reactor, 14, 20, 22
employee benchmarks/goals, 11, 97,
  158–59, 162
  quarterly, 159
  timelines for, 159
employee challenging of policy or
  rules, 161–62
  consistency by manager and, 162
  persistence by manager and, 162
  repeating of rules, 162
employee discipline, 179, 200–201,
  206, 210
  challenging of policy or rules,
    161–62
employee handbook. *See* policies
  and procedures manual or
  handbook
employee lateness, 83, 99, 162, 163,
  165–66
  changing lateness habit, 119

things that cause lateness, 118
  See also time issues
employee performance reviews, 10,
  12, 160, 162, 170
  annual, 160
  consequences for negative
    behavior, 161, 162, 166,
    200–201, 206, 210
  promotions, basis of, 199, 205,
    209, 212
  rewards for positive behavior,
    160–61, 188, 198–99, 204,
    209, 211–12
Empty Pit coworker, 73, 77–78, 83,
  92–93, 99, 100
  unhooking from, 93–94
Entertainer role, xiii, 48, 52–53
  unhooking from, 63–65, 71
equipment
  anticipating reliability of, 114–15
  break-down as predictable
    problem, 114
Exploder boss, 73, 76–77, 83,
  90–91, 99, 100
  unhooking from, 91–92

F
Fatal Attractions at work, xiv, xvi,
  73–102
  the Absentee boss, 128, 145–46
  advanced four-step unhooking
    techniques for, 86–90
  boss, relationship with, 74–75,
    139–55
  Chip on the Shoulder employee,
    73, 82–83, 84, 97–98, 99, 102
  Chip on the Shoulder employee,
    unhooking from, 98–99
  the Controlling Egomaniac boss,
    128, 141–45
  the Credit Stealer boss, 151–54
  deal with, 90, 91, 93, 95, 96–97,
    98, 100, 101, 102, 145, 148,
    151, 153–54, 155

depersonalizing, 89–90, 91, 93, 95, 96, 98, 100, 101, 102, 144–45, 147–48, 150–51, 153, 155

detaching from, 88, 91, 92, 95, 96, 98, 100, 101, 102, 144, 147, 150, 153, 155

detach test, 89

Empty Pit coworker or employee, 73, 77–78, 83, 92–93, 99, 100

Empty Pit, unhooking from, 93–94

expect to be tested, 99–100

Exploder boss, 73, 76–77, 83, 90–91, 99, 100

Exploder boss, unhooking from, 91–92

extreme bosses as, 139–55

identifying (detecting), 76–84, 86–88, 90–91, 92, 94, 96, 97–98, 100, 101, 102, 144, 147, 150, 153, 155

Pedestal Smasher boss, 73, 80–81, 83, 96–97, 99, 101

Pedestal Smasher boss, unhooking from, 97

Saboteur coworker, 73, 78–80, 83, 94–95, 99, 101

Saboteur coworker, unhooking from, 95–96

seven stages, 84–86, 140

the Unpleasable boss, 148–51

as vicious cycle, 86

food (in the workplace), 45

G

gatekeeping, 120–21, 126

H

Hero role, xiii, 48, 49–50

unhooking from, 55–57, 70

hooked (experience of being caught in an emotionally distressing situation), 2

emotional hooks, typical, 2

emotional reactions, 4, 13–14, 20, 22

identifying experience of, 5, 13–15, 19

mental reactions, 4, 14, 20, 22

physical reactions, 4, 13, 20, 22

roles at work and, 47

warning signs that you may be hooked, 22

workplace dissatisfaction and, 3, 194

See also unhooking

I

incompetence as irritant, xii, 105–6, 107–8, 128, 134–37, 154

Invisible Man (or Woman) role, xiii, 48, 54–55

unhooking from, 67–69, 72

J

job descriptions, 10, 11, 93, 158, 162, 163

K

keeping one's word, 27–28, 34–36, 46

L

language (foul, offensive, off-color) in the workplace, 45

M

Madonna, 48

management changes and job dissatisfaction, 214–16

management headaches, 163–79, 192

the Addict, 165, 176–78

the Attention Seeker, 164, 172–73

the Bad Attitude, 164, 173–75

management headaches (continued)
  the Chronically Delayed, 163, 165–66
  the Cynic, 164, 168–70
  the MIA (Missing in Action), 163, 166–68
  the Passive-Aggressive, 164, 170–72
  the Slug, 164, 175–76
  the Thief, 165, 178–79
management shoulds, 157, 179–91, 192–92
  employees should behave the way I do, 157, 180, 181–82, 192
  employees should get along with one another, 157, 180, 189–90, 193
  employees should know that I appreciate them, 157, 180, 187–88, 193
  employees should know what I need, 157, 180, 185–86, 193
  employees should like and appreciate me, 157, 180, 186–87, 193
  employees shouldn't challenge me, 157, 180, 190–91, 193
  employees shouldn't make mistakes, 157, 180, 182–83, 192
  employees should prioritize their work, 157, 180, 184–85, 193
  I shouldn't have to be their parent, 157, 180, 183–84, 192
  I should say things once, 157, 180–81, 192
  Supervisory Should inventory, 181, 182, 183, 184, 185, 186, 187, 188, 189–90
management styles, 199, 204–5, 209, 212
managers, xv, xvi, xvii
  business parenting, 156–93 (see also managing down: business parenting)

business tools for, 10–13
Chip on the Shoulder employee, dealing with, 82–83, 97–99
crisis management, 200, 206, 209, 212
decision-making style, 200, 205–6, 209
meeting with employees, xv, 108–10, 117, 125, 134
setting an emotional expression boundary, 37–39
styles of, 199, 204–5, 209, 212
unhooking from hostile employee, 17–19
managing down: business parenting, 156–93
employee negative behavior, consequences for, 161, 166
employee rewards, 160–61, 188, 198–99, 204, 209, 211–12
four key principles of business parenting (summary), 156, 191–92
goals and benchmarks for employees, 158–59
job descriptions, 10, 11, 93, 158, 162, 163
nine management headaches, 163–79, 192 (see also management headaches, main entry)
performance reviews, 10, 12, 160, 162, 170
policies and procedures (P&P) manuals, 159–60, 162, 166
principle #1: employees need to know what is expected of them, 158–60, 166, 167, 169, 171, 172–73, 174, 176, 178
principle #2: employees need consistent feedback, 160–61, 166, 168, 169, 171, 173, 174, 176, 178
principle #3:employees will test

their environment, 161–62, 166, 168, 169–70, 171, 173, 174, 176, 178

principle #4: business tools are a manager's best friends, 162–63, 166, 168, 171–72, 173, 174, 176, 178

staff meetings, 162, 163, 174 (*see also* meetings)

ten supervisory shoulds that prevent managers from interacting effectively with their staff, 157, 179–91, 192 (*see also* management shoulds)

managing up, 103–26

accepting your boss has limitations, 107–8

five pivotal practices (summary), 103

high five (summary, advanced practices), 103, 126

high five #1: be on time or early to start the day, 118–19, 126

high five #2: be a gatekeeper and keep time-eaters away, 120, 126

high five #3: create systems so that your boss can find things if you're not around, 121–22, 126

high five #4: keep confidential information where it belongs, 122–23, 126

high five #5: underpromise and overdeliver, 124–25, 126

normalizing predictable problems, 114

pivotal practice #1: train your boss to meet with you regularly, 108–10, 117, 125, 134

pivotal practice #2: come to every meeting with a detailed agenda, 110–12, 117, 125

pivotal practice #3: keep a pulse on your boss's changing priorities, 112–13, 125

pivotal practice #4: anticipate problems and offer solutions, 113–15

pivotal practice #5: always be prepared to give status reports on your projects at any time, 115–16, 117, 125

poor managers, reasons for, 105–6

problem prevention actions, 114–15

questions to ask your boss on daily priorities, 113

symptoms and treatments, 125

taking responsibility for improving the relationship, 108

manners/courtesy in the workplace, 29–30, 39–40, 44, 46

Martyr role, 47, 52

unhooking from, 62–63, 71

meetings

agenda, come to every meeting with a detailed, 110–11, 117, 125

agenda, sample, 111

agenda, sticking to, 112

boss cancels, xiv, 104, 117

bringing documentation to, 110

lateness for, xii

negative emotional reaction to, 3–4, 109

staff, 162, 163, 174

train your boss to meet with you regularly, xv, 108–10, 117, 125

your voice not heard at, xiii, 54–55, 68, 72

mental reactor, 14, 20, 22

micromanagers, 142

moral code or value system, 202, 207, 210, 213

N

noise in the workplace, xii, 30, 46
   coworker who oversteps noise
      boundary, 40–42

P

Passive-Aggressive-type employee,
   164, 170–72
Peacemaker role, 48, 53–54
   unhooking from, 65–67, 71
Pedestal Smasher-type boss, 73,
   80–81, 83, 96–97, 99, 101
   unhooking from, 97
personal hygiene in the workplace,
   45
personal information, sharing of,
   xii, 28, 46
   boss who oversteps personal
      information boundary, 36–37
   Caregiver role and, 50–51
personal space in the office, xii,
   26–27, 33–34, 46
   physical contact, unwanted, 27
physical activities that release
      negative energy, 22
   focus on your breath, 6, 7, 41,
      91, 93, 98–99
   health clubs and, 7, 36, 98
   massage, 33, 130
   meditation, 97
   nature, spending time in, 133
   rigorous exercise (and walking),
      6, 16, 18, 32, 41, 95, 136
   splashing cold water on your
      face, 6
   visualization, 93
   yoga class, 40
physical reactor, 13, 20, 22
policies and procedures (P&P)
      manual or handbook, 11, 39,
      159–60, 162, 166
   company rule enforcement, 162,
      200–201, 206, 210

dress code in, 159, 160
politics in the workplace, 201, 207,
   210, 213
Porras, Jerry I., 194
Powell, Colin, 48
promotions, basis of, 199, 205, 209,
   212

Q

qualities, personal and ethical,
      prized by employer (list), 198,
      203–4, 208, 211
   rewarded by advancement , 201,
      209, 213
quitting a job
   the Absentee boss and, 148
   bad corporate fit and, 213
   the Controlling Egomaniac boss
      and, 145
   the Credit Stealing boss and,
      154
   the Unpleasable boss and, 151
quiz on workplace challenges,
   xii–xv

R

Rebel/Scapegoat role, 48, 51–52
   unhooking from, 59–62, 70
relationships with boss or
      coworkers. *See* Fatal
      Attractions at work
reward system, 160–61, 188,
   198–99, 204, 209, 211–12
roles in the workplace, xvi, 47–72
   becoming branded, 49
   Caregiver, 48, 50–51, 77–78
   Caregiver, unhooking from role,
      58–59, 70
   Dumping Ground, xiii
   Entertainer, xiii, 48, 52–53
   Entertainer, unhooking from
      role, 63–65, 71
   Hero, xiii, 48, 49–50

Hero, unhooking from role,
55–57, 70
how to unhook from, 47
identifying your role, 49–55
Invisible Man (or Woman), xiii,
48, 54–55
Invisible One, unhooking from
role, 67–69, 72
limitation by, self-test, 48
Martyr, 47, 52
Martyr, unhooking from role,
62–63, 71
Peacemaker, 48, 53–54
Peacemaker, unhooking from
role, 65–67, 71
Rebel/Scapegoat, 48, 51–52
Rebel, unhooking from role,
59–62, 70
taking on the part, 49
Target, xiii
unhooking, steps for, 55–69

S
Saboteur-type coworker, 73, 78–80,
83, 94–95, 99, 101
unhooking from, 95–96
Sacred Cow-type boss, 128, 134–37,
154
Shoot-the-Messenger-type boss,
128, 131–34, 154
Slug-type employee, 164, 175–76
smells in the workplace, 45
status reports, 115–16, 117, 125
content, 116
stress at work
corporate culture and level of,
202, 207, 210, 213
healthy ways to release negative
energy, 6–7, 16, 18, 22, 32,
33, 36, 40, 41, 91, 93, 95, 97,
98–99, 130, 133, 136
reactions to, xii
unhealthy forms of releasing
negative energy, 7

systems, creation of by employee,
121–22, 126

T
thievery by employee, 164, 178–79
time cushions, 119
time-eaters, 120–21, 126
time issues
arriving on time, enforcing rule,
162
being on time or early to start
the day, 118–19, 126
boundary problems with
(lateness, failure to appear),
xii, 26, 32–33, 46
changing lateness habit, 119
the chronically late employee,
163, 165–66
things that cause lateness, 118
trading favors, 138, 139

U
unhooking (changing your reaction
to a hook), xvi, 4–10
from boss, the Avoider type,
129–31
from boss, Charming, Cheating
Liar (CCL), 137–39
from boss, conflicts with, 15–17
from boss, the Sacred Cow type,
136–37
from boss, Shoot-the-Messenger
type, 133–34
from boss who oversteps personal
information boundary, 36–37
business tool for, 5, 6, 10–13, 17,
19, 21, 22, 33, 34, 36, 37, 39,
40, 42, 92, 93, 95–96, 97,
131, 136–37
from Caregiver role, 58–59, 70
consequences of setting
boundaries, 43–44
from coworker who doesn't keep
his word, 34–36

unhooking (changing your reaction to a hook) (*continued*)

from coworker who is rude, 39–40, 44

from coworker who oversteps noise boundary, 40–42

from coworker who oversteps space boundary, 33–34, 44

from customer who oversteps time boundary, 32–33, 43–44

from employee who is hostile, 17–19

from employee who oversteps an emotional expression boundary, 37–39

from Entertainer role, 63–65, 71

from Fatal Attractions, advanced four-step unhooking technique for, 86–90

from Fatal Attractions, unhooking from, 91–102

four-pronged unhooking technique, 22

from Hero role, 55–57, 70

high-road vs. low-road communication, 9–10, 42–43

from Invisible One role, 67–69, 72

from Martyr role, 62–63, 71

mental inventory, questions to ask yourself, 8–9, 16–17, 18, 20–21, 32–33, 34, 35, 37, 38, 40, 41–42, 130–31, 133, 136, 138–39

mentally unhooking, 5, 8–9, 16, 22, 92, 93, 95, 97

from Peacemaker role, 65–67, 71

physically unhooking, 5, 6–7, 16, 18, 20, 22, 32, 33, 35, 36, 38, 41, 91, 93, 95, 97, 130, 133, 136, 138

from Rebel role, 59–62, 70

unhealthy forms of releasing negative energy, 7

verbally unhooking, 5, 9–10, 17, 19, 21, 22, 33, 34, 35–36, 37, 42, 92, 93, 95, 97, 131, 134, 136, 139

your personal unhooking assessment, 19–21

See also business toolbox; physical activities to release negative energy

Unpleasable boss, 128, 148–51, 155

W

Williams, Robin, 48

work environment

dissatisfaction with, three examples, 195–96

general type of, 197, 202, 208, 211, 216–17

identifying compatible, xvi, 194–221

moral code, 202, 207, 210, 213

physical setting, 196

politics in, 201, 207, 210, 213

See also corporate culture

write-ups and warnings, 162, 169

About the Authors

Harvard-trained psychotherapist KATHERINE CROWLEY and nationally recognized business strategist KATHI ELSTER have developed a method for dealing with difficult people and challenging conditions at work. Published authors, college educators, public speakers, and veteran consultants, Katherine and Kathi are seasoned guides in the area of professional fulfillment through self-awareness and self-management.

Their successful company, K Squared Enterprises, is dedicated to helping individuals and companies accomplish their business objectives while navigating the psychological challenges of working with others. Since 1989, they've helped hundreds of companies by training thousands of individuals in their time-tested methodology.

K Squared Enterprises
119 West 23rd St, Suite 1009
New York, NY 10011
Phone: (212) 929-7676
Fax: (212) 929-6655
www.workingwithyouiskillingme.com